BARTON

A Young Person's Guide
to
Art in Australia

First published 1986 by
THE MACMILLAN COMPANY OF AUSTRALIA PTY LTD
107 Moray Street, South Melbourne 3205

Associated companies and representatives
throughout the world

National Library of Australia
cataloguing in publication data

A Young Person's Guide To Art In Australia

Includes Index.
ISBN 0 333 41542 6.

1. Art Appreciation — Juvenile Literature.
701'.1

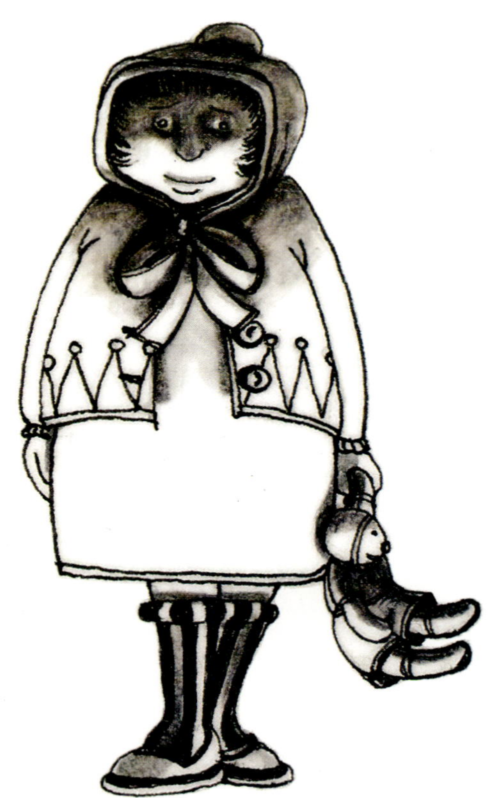

Designed by Marcos Maureira
Typeset by Band News, Sydney
Printed in Singapore

A Young Person's Guide
to
Art in Australia

Consulting Editor: R*obin Norling*

Contributors: *Peter Roach*
Alexandra Towle
Simon Blackall

Illustrations by Drahos Zak

This project was assisted by the Visual Arts Board of the Australia Council,
the Federal Government's arts funding and advisory body.

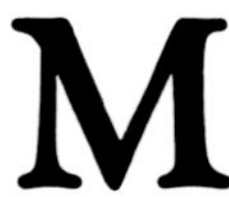

Contents

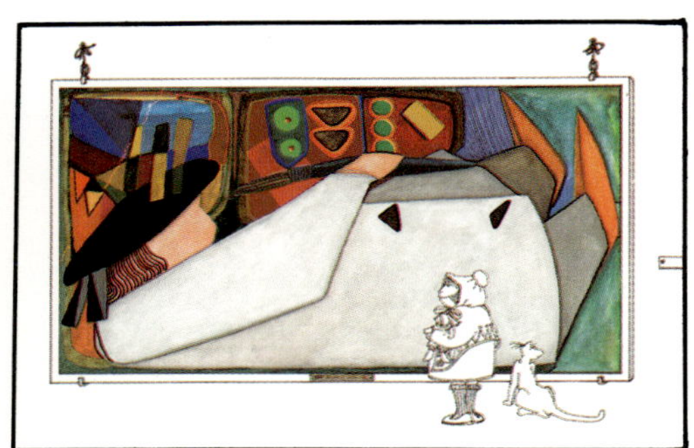

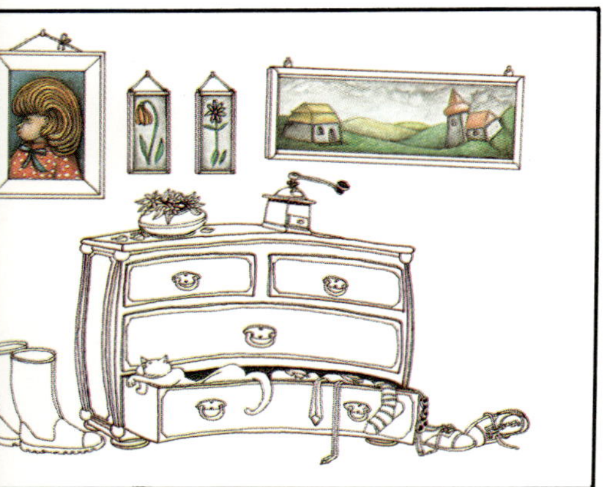

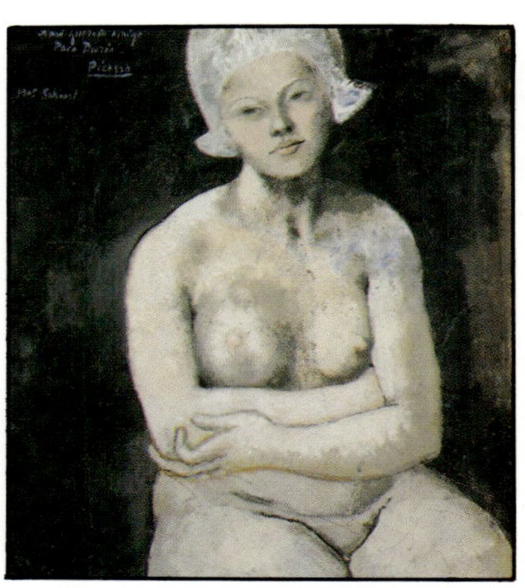

INTRODUCTION

This book is about appreciation. Not just the basic pleasures of seeing things that are pleasing or beautiful, but something more.

Here you can learn how to get the extra pleasure that comes from understanding the details of paintings, finding out what goes into making them and knowing how they have changed from age to age.

Much of the skill of appreciation (knowing/looking) is gained by slowing down and understanding what a picture is about. The extra time you spend looking at a picture will be well worth while.

No single book can·tell you everything about a painting; what the artist was thinking when he or she painted that picture, what you might think or feel when you look at it, or what caused this particular 'visual thought' to happen. The aim of this book is to start you thinking about these things, to help you understand that a painting is always a statement — it is always more than a two-dimensional object hanging on a wall.

This book will help you to enjoy both realistic and abstract art. The examples in this book range from a simple drawing made in a cave in Queensland many thousands of years ago to paintings from the present day. Nearly all of these paintings are on view in the major public galleries of Australia.

It is always enjoyable to look at reproductions in a book, but it is much better to see and enjoy the real thing. We hope that this book will inspire you to learn about and appreciate the wealth of art available to you in Australia.

VISITING AN ART GALLERY

When you have an opportunity to go to an art gallery, try to make your visit as memorable as possible. Here are a few basic hints which will help you get the maximum amount of pleasure from your trip.

KNOW WHAT TO SEE

Firstly, it is important to know what is on view in the gallery. Nearly all galleries have printed guide books about their collections of paintings and often they will include details of each picture and sometimes stories about the painter. A short time spent studying the guide can often help you to appreciate a picture far more than you would by suddenly coming to it after seeing possibly hundreds of others. Some galleries even lease out tape recorders with pre-recorded cassettes of information about each painting, though this usually costs money.

DON'T TRY TO SEE TOO MUCH

There is no way you can 'do' an art gallery in an hour or even a day. Don't attempt it! Choose two or three paintings that you think you might enjoy and be prepared to sit with each one for a while and have a conversation with it. Find out (by studying the picture) the things that interest that particular artist — maybe it is light or colour or texture — and see if they are the same things that interest you. How is your idea or memory different? Find out the artist's slant on life, their bias or viewpoint (e.g. hates cats/feels small/ loves brown, etc). The answers are usually there before your eyes.

STUDY THE PAINTING

When you stop in front of a picture, look for those things we have described in this book. Think what materials have been used; the way light and shade influence mood; how

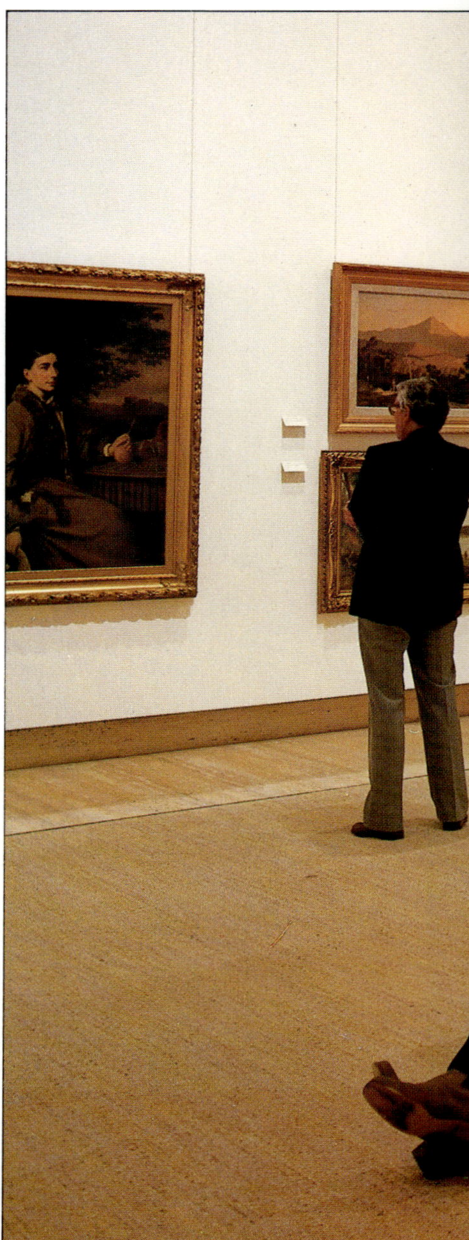

Queensland Art Gallery, Brisbane

perspective is used; and try to understand the message the artist is trying to convey to you about the country, the person, the place or the time when the painting was made.

Most art galleries put on special exhibitions from time to time. These exhibitions give you a chance to see collections of paintings brought together from other galleries all over Australia. Sometimes these exhibitions may even have been brought from overseas, giving you a once-in-a-lifetime opportunity of seeing and understanding the scope and breadth of an artist's work.

Don't leave an art gallery as if you are closing a book. Most art galleries have small shops or sales counters where you can buy books, prints and postcards. A good idea is to buy postcards of your favourite paintings to keep as reminders or to send to friends.

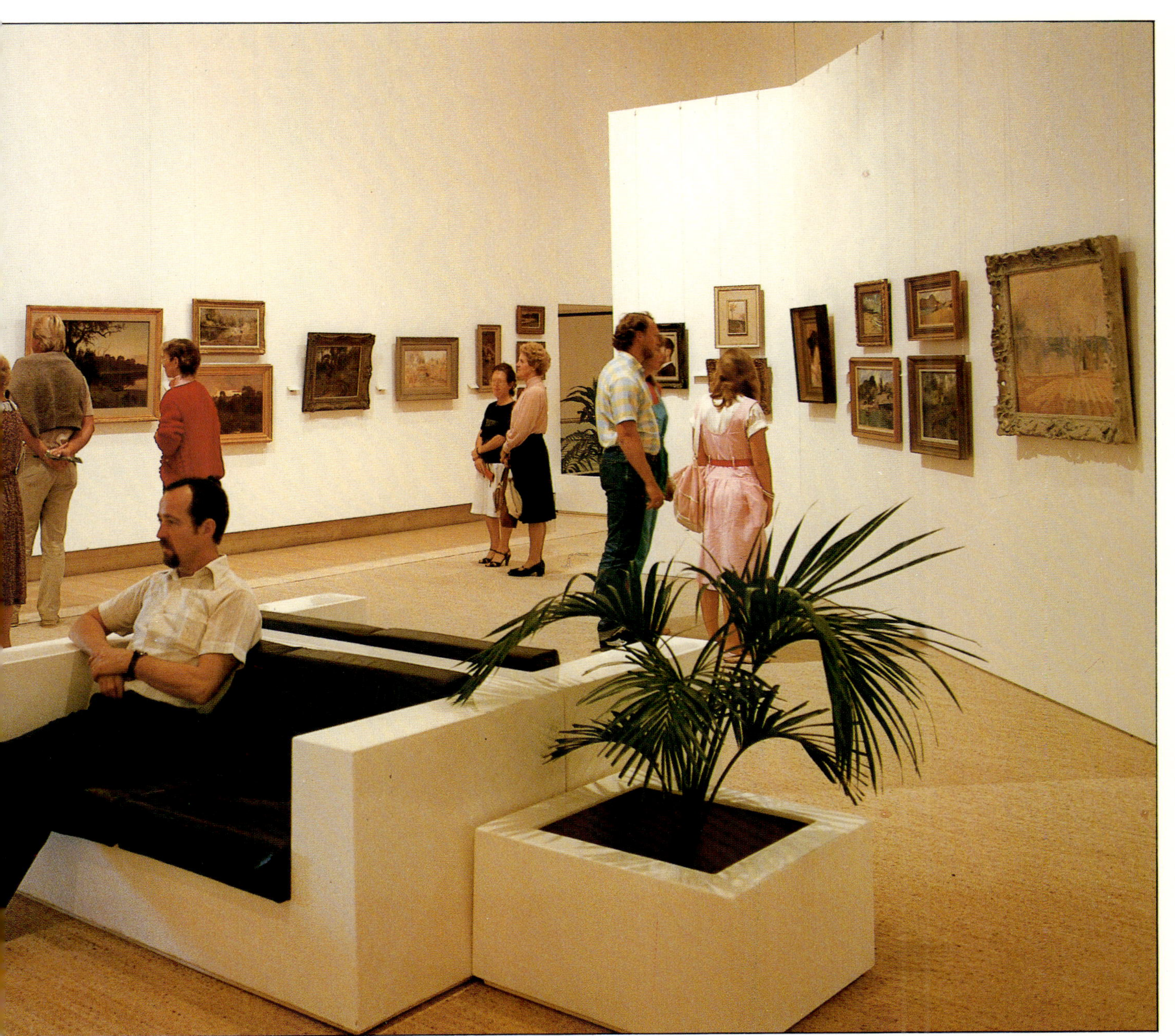

It is often said that the land and not its people moulds the character of a nation. The same could be said about painting. The unique qualities of each country are usually reflected in landscape painting. Although most of us live in cities around the coastline of Australia, if we look at a map or drive to another city we are constantly reminded of the vastness and diversity of the Australian bush. The sheer size of the country, its variety of different colours and the brightness of our daylight are features which make Australia very different from other parts of the world. They are also features which have moulded Australian landscape painting.

Mills Plain *1836*
John Glover *1767 — 1847*
(English / Australian)
Oil on canvas
76.2 x 151.9 cm
Tasmanian Museum and
Art Gallery, Hobart

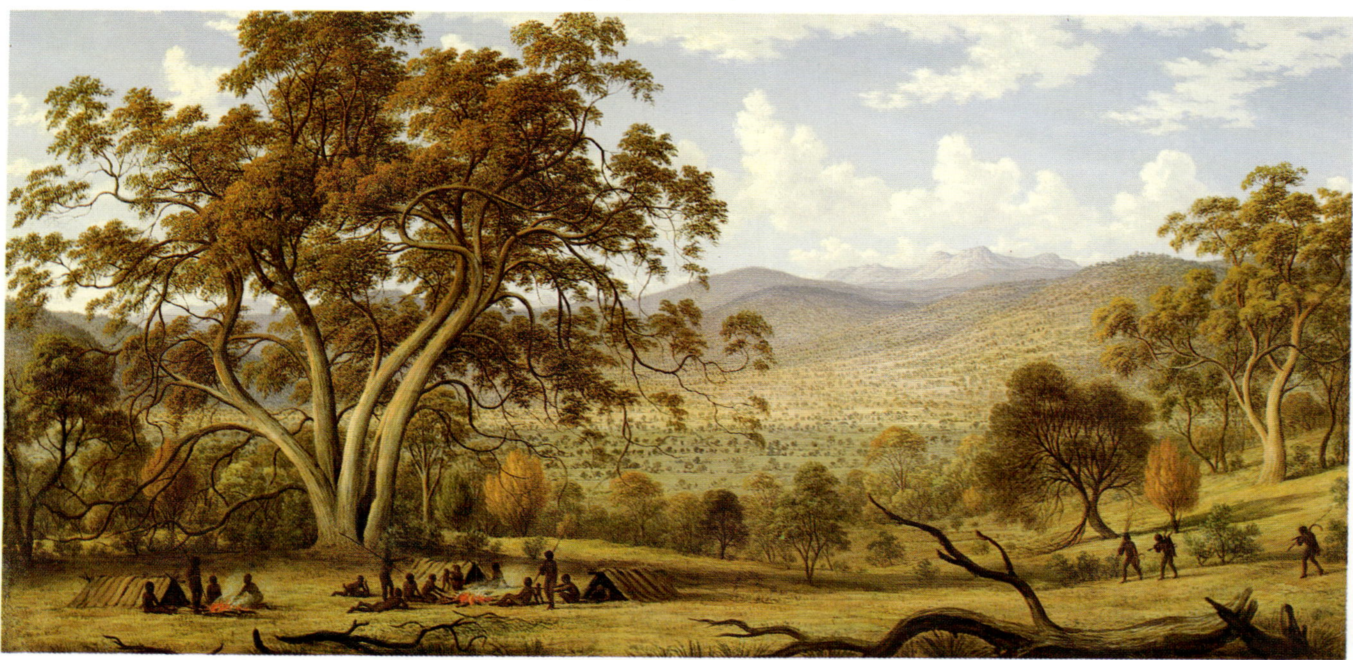

JOHN GLOVER was an English artist who became one of the pioneers of Australian landscape painting. He was a respected artist in England before he moved to Van Diemen's Land (now Tasmania), where he was given a large grant of land to farm. Glover painted many scenes of the land around his property. *Mills Plains*, painted in 1836, is typical of his work. It is very realistic and just like the landscape around Deddington where he lived. In the foreground we see a group of Aborigines. The large group of mountains in the background is Ben Lomond, a mountain range that dominates the landscape of this region.

Glover was more interested in painting highly-detailed landscapes than capturing the atmosphere of the new land. His fine brush work, draughtsmanship and strong sense of formal composition were characteristic of the landscape-painting traditions of Europe. He would often bracket a scene with trees, anchor one side of a painting with a building or introduce a group of people to the foreground to hold our attention. Glover saw Van Diemen's Land as an extension of the peaceful rural settings of his native England rather than the wilderness it really was.

EUGEN VON GUERARD was another artist who migrated to Australia. Like Glover he was an important early landscape painter. Many artists in the 19th century were influenced by scientific explorations. They wanted to look carefully at nature and make precise notes of their observations. It was for this reason that von Guerard accompanied a scientist on an expedition to Mount Kosciusko, Australia's highest mountain. The scientist was Professor von Neumayer who was making a magnetic survey of the Snowy Mountains. In this picture of Mount Kosciusko, painted in 1863, von Guerard depicts the professor setting up some equipment with the aid of an assistant and his dog Hector, against the rugged terrain of the southern ranges of NSW.

Von Guerard was also meticulous when it came to painting detail. His landscapes depict the broad sweep and majesty of nature. These panoramas combine the finest traditions of European landscape painting with their formal approach to composition. In *Mount Kosciusko* von Guerard places his figures towards the bottom left of the picture. They are minute against the large cluster of boulders but they still centre our attention so the eye can move freely over the rhythmic formation of rocks and peaks which form the middle ground and background. To heighten scale and perspective, sunlight blazes through clouds onto the middle ground, which is covered in melting ice, while the foreground remains in shadow.

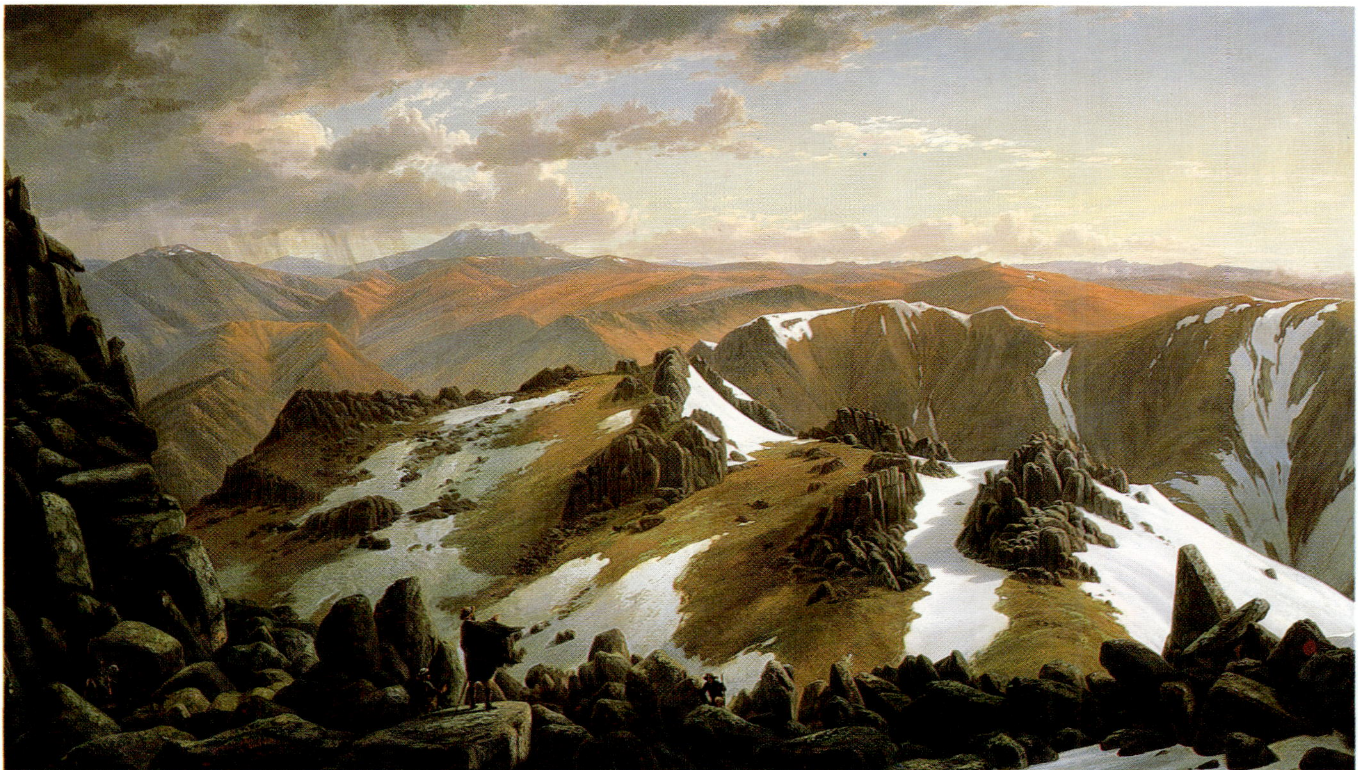

Mount Kosciusko 19 November *1867*
Johann Joseph Eugen von Guerard *1812 — 1901 (Austrian/Australian)*
Oil on canvas
66.2 x 117 cm
Australian National Gallery, Canberra

CLAUDE MONET was an important French artist often described as 'the painter of light'. He was a founding member of the Impressionist movement which began in France in the 1880s. The artists in the movement placed great importance on painting outdoors and believed that art should accurately record the impact of light on landscape. Monet once said that 'my only virtue is to have painted directly in front of nature, while trying to depict the impressions made on me by the most fleeting effects.' In this painting Monet shows us a brief moment when the sun, low in the sky, lights up the haystacks from behind, giving them a halo of light. For Monet detail was not important, but mood and atmosphere were. To create the impression of a landscape shimmering with light, Monet used thick, expressive brush strokes.

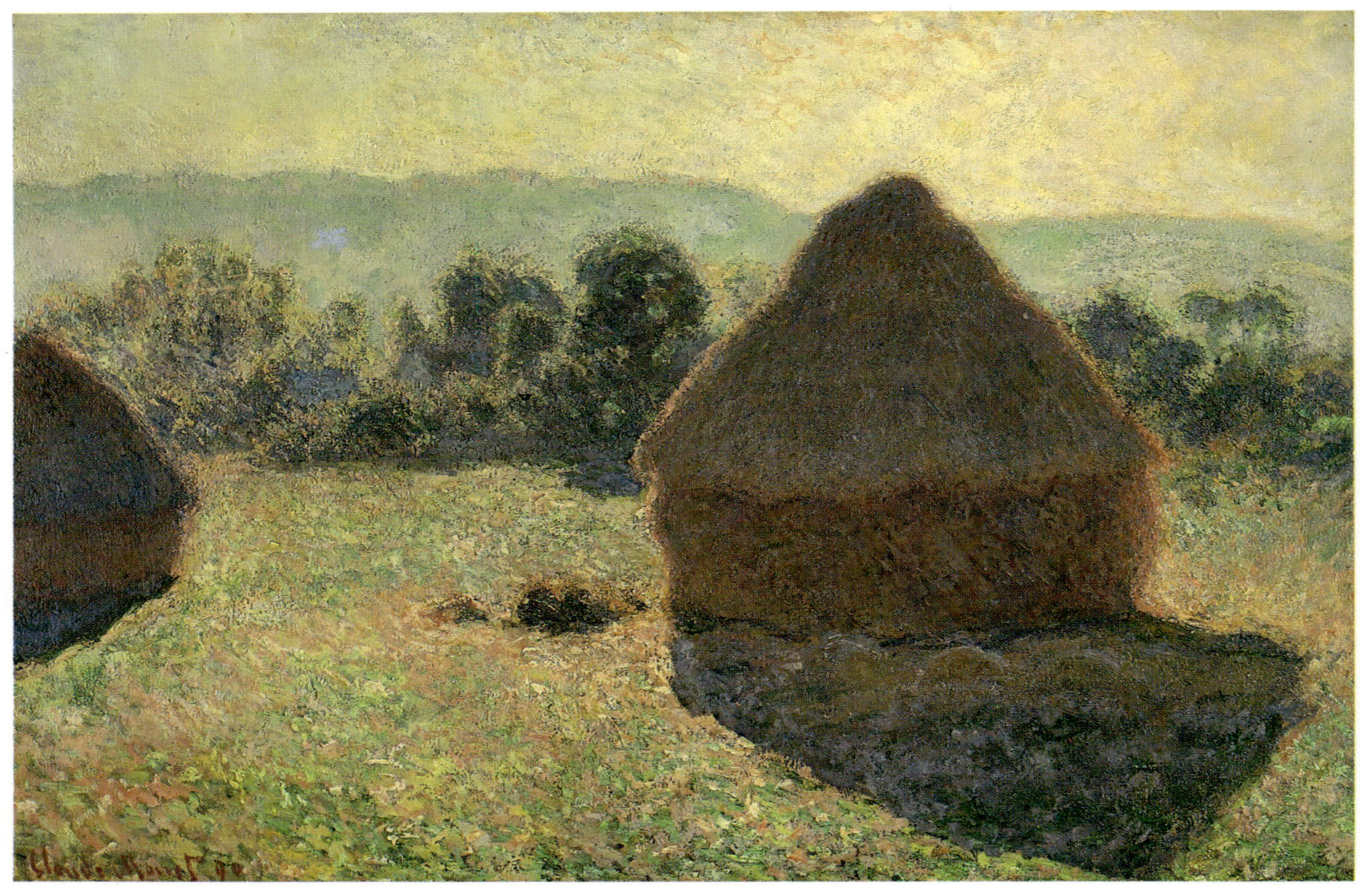

Haystacks at Noon *1890*
Claude Monet *1840 — 1890 (French)*
Oil on canvas
65.8 x 101cm
Australian National Gallery, Canberra

FRED WILLIAMS made a major contribution to Australian landscape painting. He reduced the landscape to a minimum number of simple forms. These forms denote trees or rocks and are either dotted or blobbed on delicately painted backgrounds. Although they often appear to be loose and randomly dispersed, Williams always placed his forms in rhythmical formations. It is as though he almost intended them to look like musical notations running across a page.

Williams used colours long associated with the Australian bush: ochres, russets, pale olive greens, pale blues and dull brick reds. By placing the horizon line at the top of the painting and using other horizontals to signify plains and riverbanks below (or sometimes not using a horizon line at all) his landscapes look as though they are seen from the air.

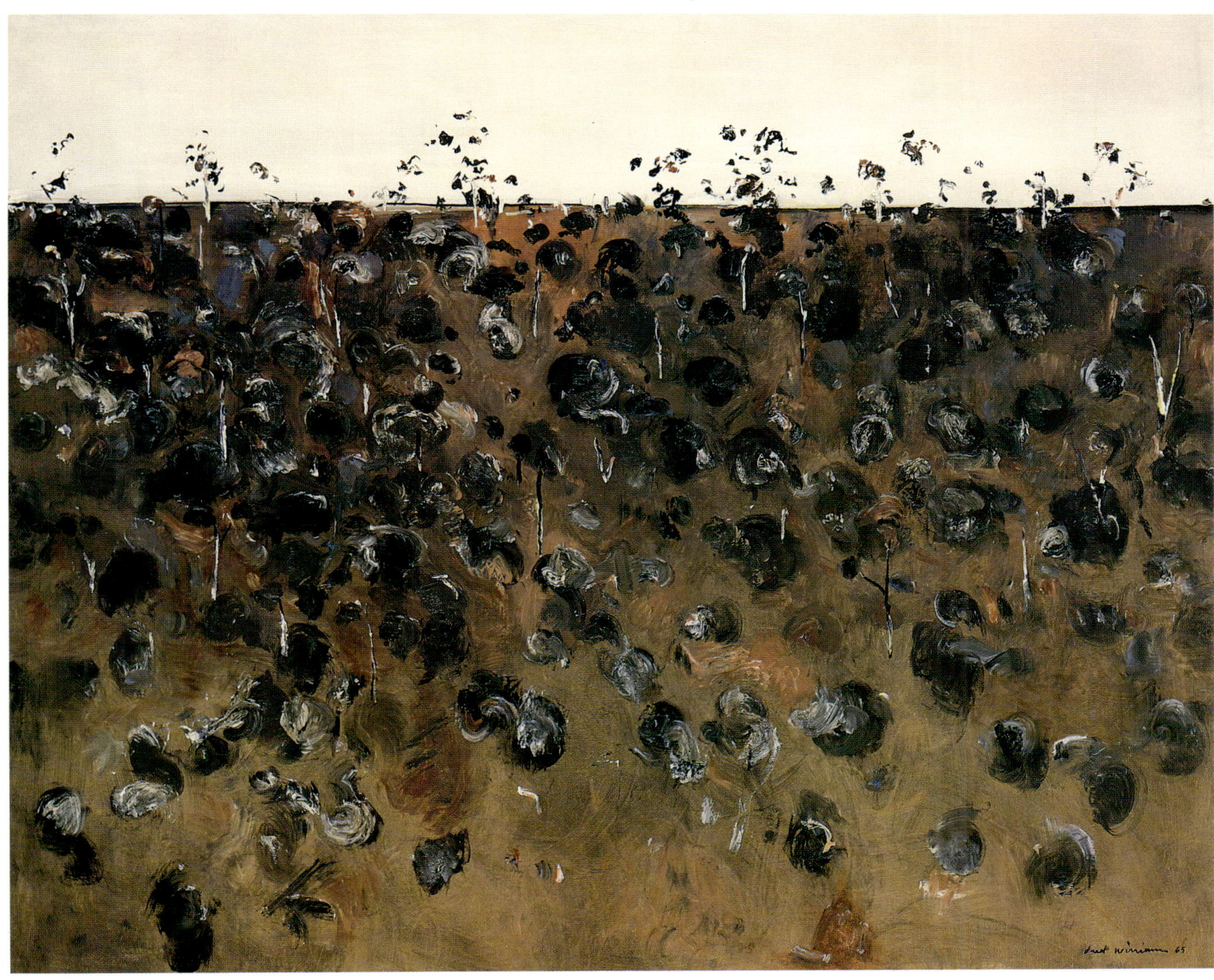

Upwey Landscape *1964/5*
Fred Williams *1927 — 1981 (Australian)*
Oil on canvas
143.3 x 182.9 cm
National Gallery of Victoria, Melbourne

Buildings, roads and street-life have always been a constant source of fascination for artists. The urban landscape of the towns and cities most of us live in provides many subjects which are interesting and worth recording. Whether it is a small alley, a detail of a shop or a panorama of a city, an artist's impression can be important to us. It can tell us a lot about our changing environment and the progress of society. For instance, it can provide an accurate historical description of the harbour of a small port before it grew into a large international city, or a bustling street with horse-drawn carriages driving by, which now has high-rise buildings and cars.

Swanston Street *1861*
Henry Burn *1807 — 1884 (Australian)*
Oil on canvas
71.5 x 91.7 cm
National Gallery of Victoria, Melbourne

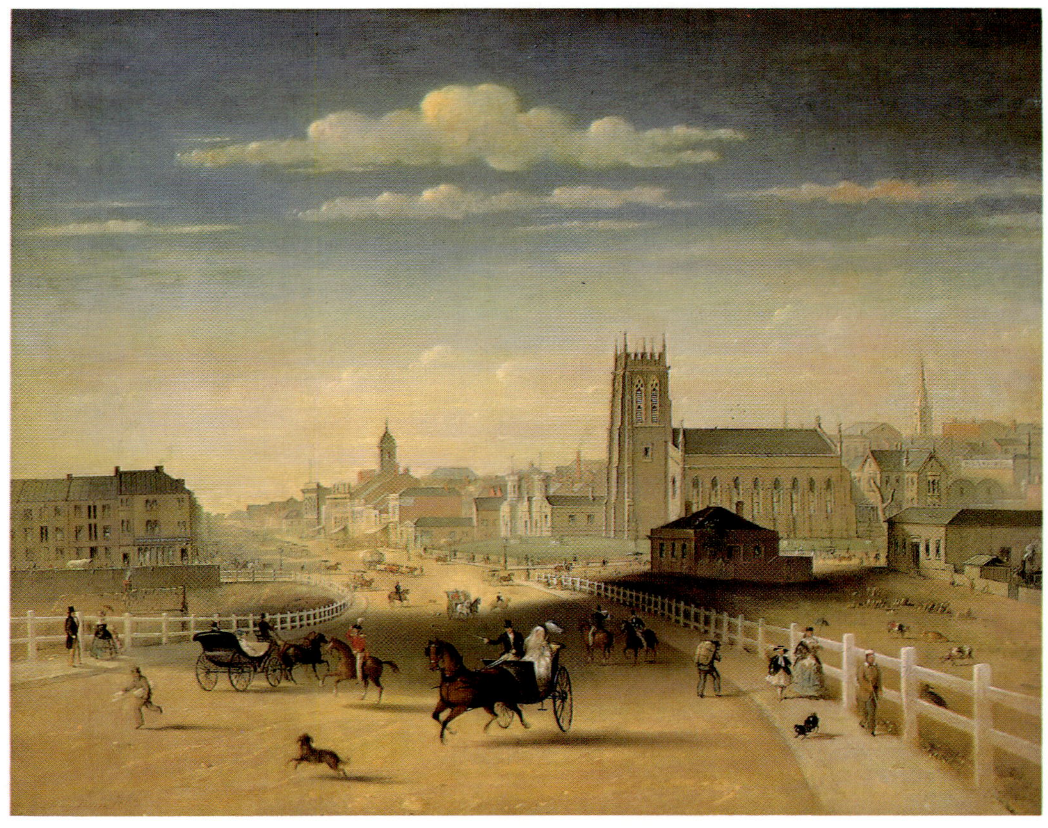

MELBOURNE was settled in 1835 and grew very rapidly, especially after the gold rush days of the 1850s. Swanston Street, now, as then, is a busy street. But over one hundred years ago it certainly looked very different. Henry Burn painted this view of Swanston Street in 1861. It shows that there were open fields with grazing cattle and only a few buildings on either side of the street. In this painting Burn uses linear perspective to increase the sense of depth. Our eye is immediately drawn up Swanston Street. We pass the open fields and the people walking in the street to the buildings in the middle ground and then to the horizon that vanishes into the low-lying sky. This dramatic use of perspective manages to make our eye travel freely as though we are about to become part of the scene.

BY THE 1880s SYDNEY had become a major Pacific port. A century before it had been little more than a penal settlement with a small convict population. Throughout the 19th century the population had grown with free settlers migrating from England to start a new life in the colonies. Many went onto the land but the majority lived in the towns and cities. Charles Conder painted this scene of Circular Quay in 1888. This painting shows Sydney as a busy port with ships calling in from all parts of the world. The grey stillness of the harbour , the low-lying clouds and the people busily walking by with umbrellas create a strong impression of a rainy day in Sydney one hundred years ago. Since this picture was painted Circular Quay has undergone many changes with high-rise development and the building of the Opera House.

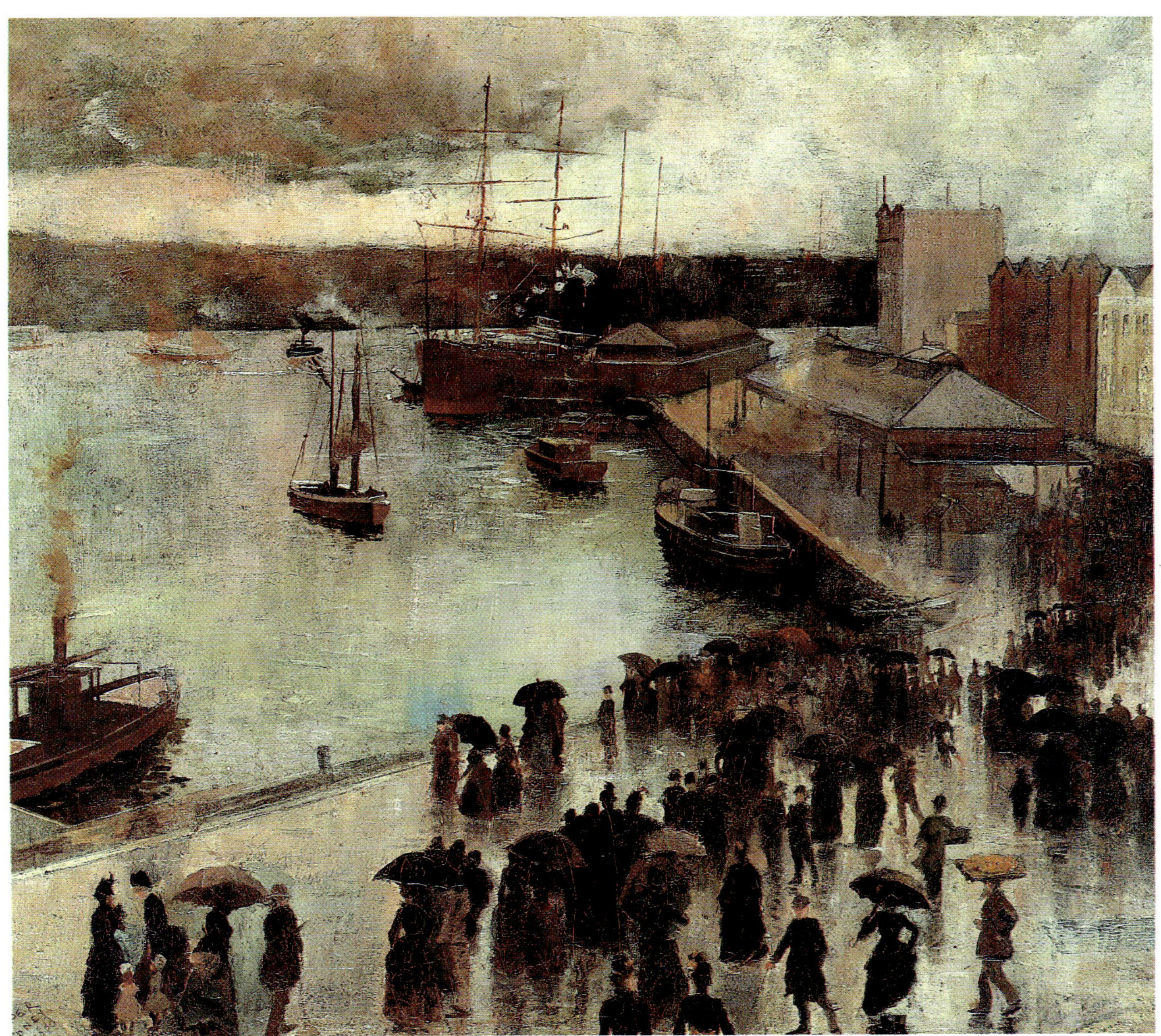

Departure of the Orient, Circular Quay *1888*
Charles Conder *1868 — 1909 (English/Australian)*
Oil on canvas
45 x 50 cm
Art Gallery of New South Wales

PORTRAITS

Everyone likes to have a record of themselves. Since ancient times, long before the discovery of photography, portrait painting was regarded as an important art form by kings and queens, political leaders and wealthy merchants. Portraits tell us a lot about people – how they live, their age, what they wear, how wealthy they are and who they are. But what makes a good portrait? Some people think that it has to be a life-like image of the sitter. Others say it has to do more with the character of a person – those special features that make the sitter a unique subject. With the introduction of photography in the 19th century, many portrait artists, not wanting to compete with the camera, moved away from life-like paintings. They began a new way of portraying people. By exaggerating the features of their subjects and treating them differently, the portrait artists were able to capture what they saw as the personalities of the sitters.

PABLO PICASSO is the best known painter of the 20th century and the greatest influence on modern art. Throughout his very long career he painted many subjects but the human form inspired him most. *La Belle Hollandaise* (also known as *The Dutch Girl with a Head-dress*) was painted in 1905 and is an earlier work of Picasso's.

This painting can be related to some of Picasso's later work which was influenced by classical Greek sculpture. By using strong contrasts of light and shade and very limited colour, the artist almost appears to carve, instead of paint, an image of the girl.

Although she is nude Picasso paints her wearing a head-dress. The head-dress is typical of the ones worn by the women of the region. Very little is known about the girl in this painting except that she was a girl he befriended on a trip to Holland, a country he very rarely visited. Picasso obviously painted this work to remind him of his stay. The girl appears very serene and relaxed. One art critic wrote that 'it was full of the most exquisite tenderness.'

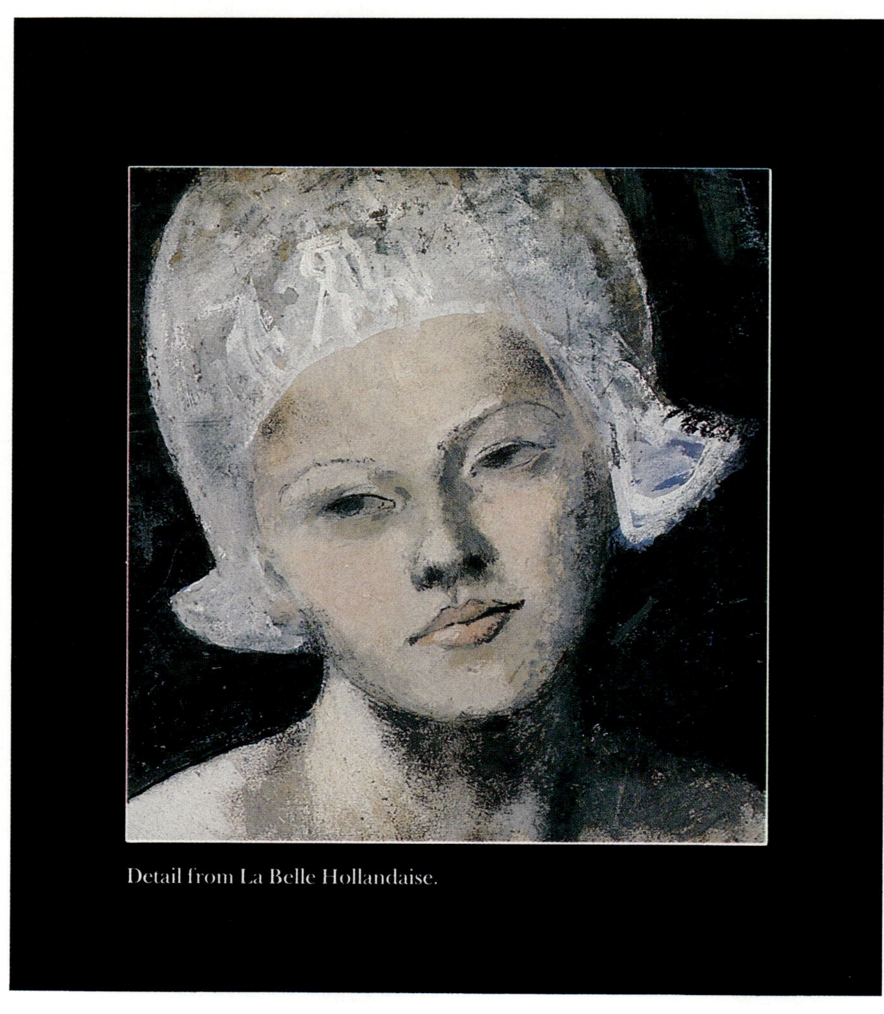

Detail from La Belle Hollandaise.

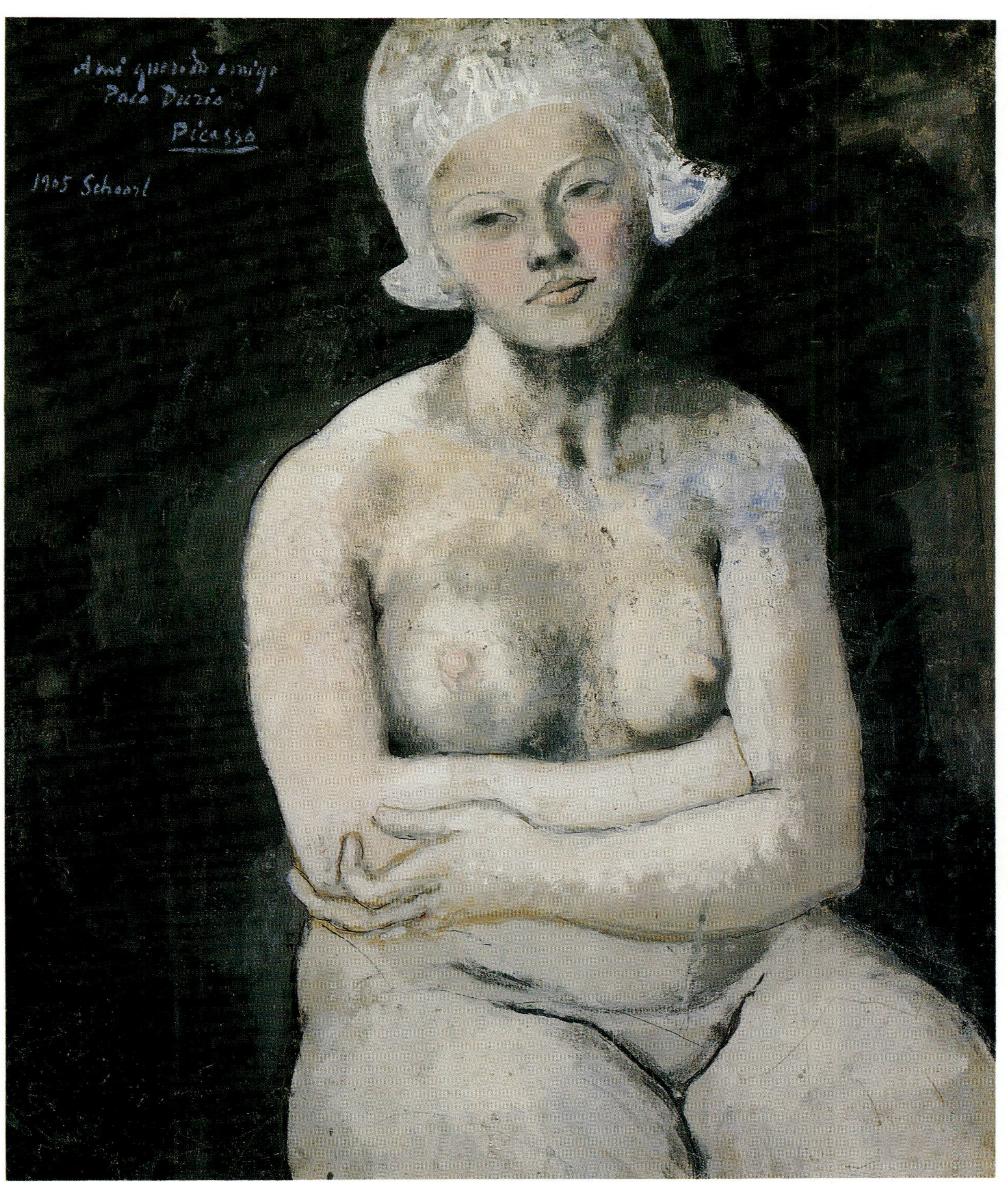

La Belle Hollandaise *1905*
Pablo Picasso *1881 — 1973 (Spanish)*
Gouache on cardboard mounted on wood
77 x 66.3 cm
Queensland Art Gallery, Brisbane

WHEN AN ARTIST paints his own portrait it is called a self-portrait. Pierre Bonnard was a famous French artist who painted portraits and many scenes of domestic life in Paris. This self-portrait was painted in 1940 when he was quite old. In this picture Bonnard is in a room filled with golden sunlight. He is concerned about painting that particular moment when the sun shines onto his face. By painting quick brushstrokes and using warm colours from pale to golden yellow, his facial features almost dissolve under the bright daylight. Like a brief sketch, we are left with only a momentary impression, but it is one that gives us a feeling of pleasure and warmth.

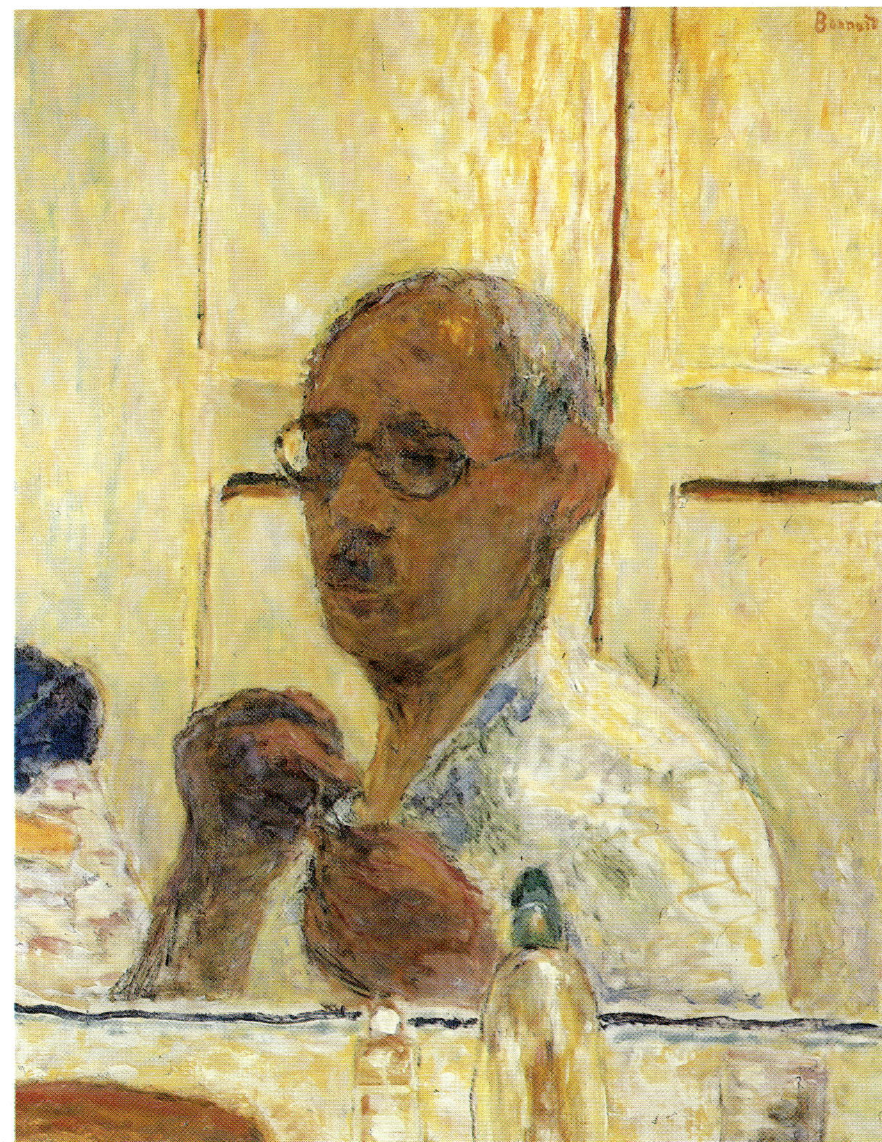

Self Portrait in Dressing Room Mirror *c. 1940*
Pierre Bonnard *1867 — 1947 (French)*
Oil on canvas
76.2 x 61 cm
Art Gallery of New South Wales

WILLIAM DOBELL is considered Australia's finest portrait painter. This painting titled *Portrait of a Strapper* is regarded as one of Dobell's most important works.
A strapper is a stable hand whose job is to groom and tend race horses. The subject for this painting was an unemployed strapper who modelled for Dobell in Sydney.

Every part of the face, neck and body of the figure in the portrait can be associated with a horse. The head is triangularly shaped like that of a horse, the hair springs up and out like a mane, the ears are big, slightly pricked up, the eyes slant and the mouth is full and prominent. The form of the figure is stretched and elongated to suggest the grace and speed of a race horse.

Technically, Dobell groomed the painting as he reworked the portrait over twelve months. The pampered treatment of the painted surface is similar to the care a strapper would show for his horse. We can see that William Dobell is a master of adapting his technique to coax out the character of his subject and that *Portrait of a Strapper* has been painted in the classic tradition of portraiture.

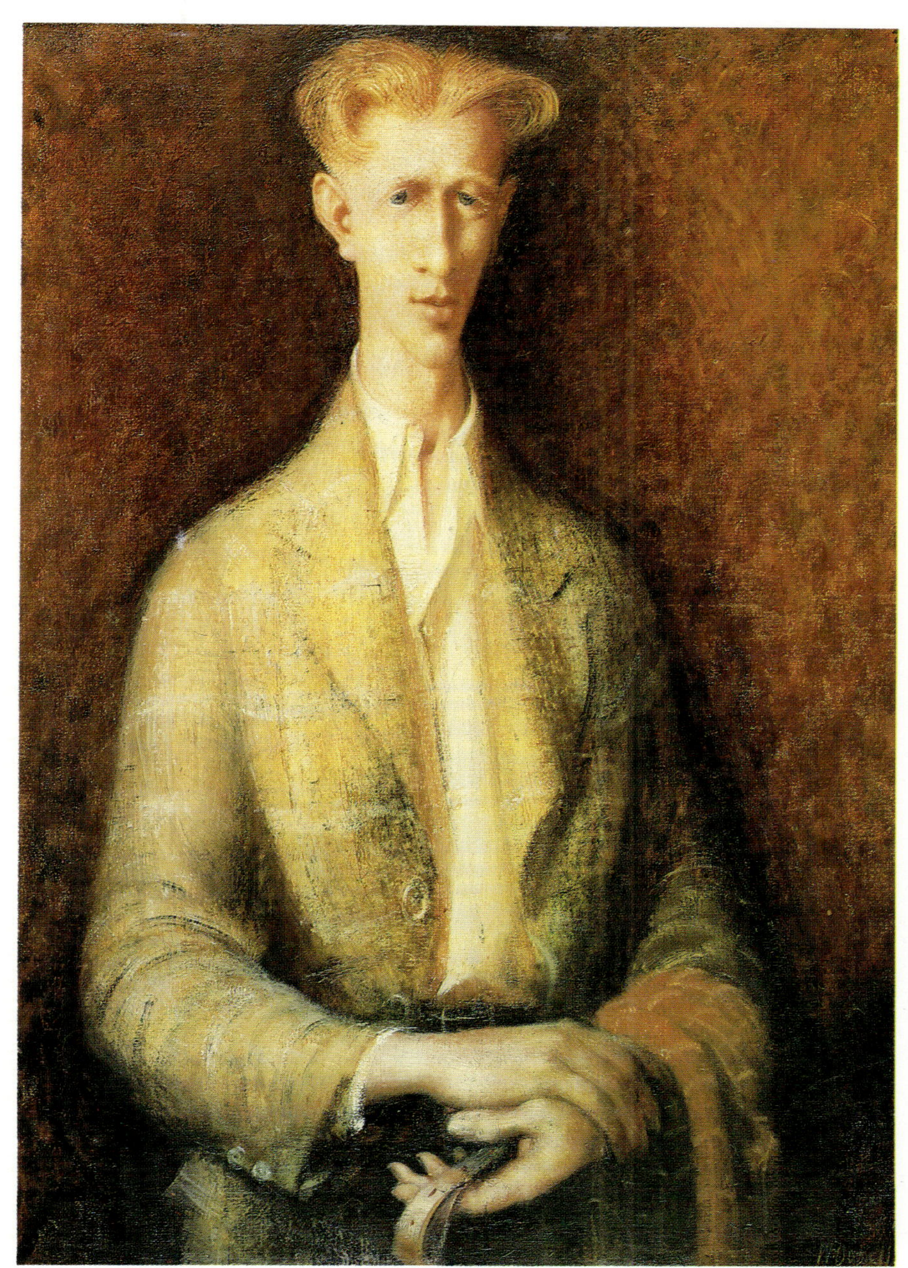

Portrait of a Strapper *1941*
William Dobell *1899 — 1970 (Australian)*
Oil on canvas
90.3 x 65.5 cm
Newcastle Region Art Gallery, Newcastle

Still life has been popular with painters for centuries because it uses familiar items we all use and know. Still life deals with everyday objects that you would find in your home such as a vase of flowers, fruit in a basket or a bottle of wine with glasses. As a subject it provides artists with a vocabulary of forms which can be painted over and over again but each time they are interpreted differently. There are many ways to paint the same thing. A glass for instance can be painted very loosely, or with incredible detail, or the artist may interpret it as being a flat, two-dimensional shape. Each view gives us a new look at a familiar object.

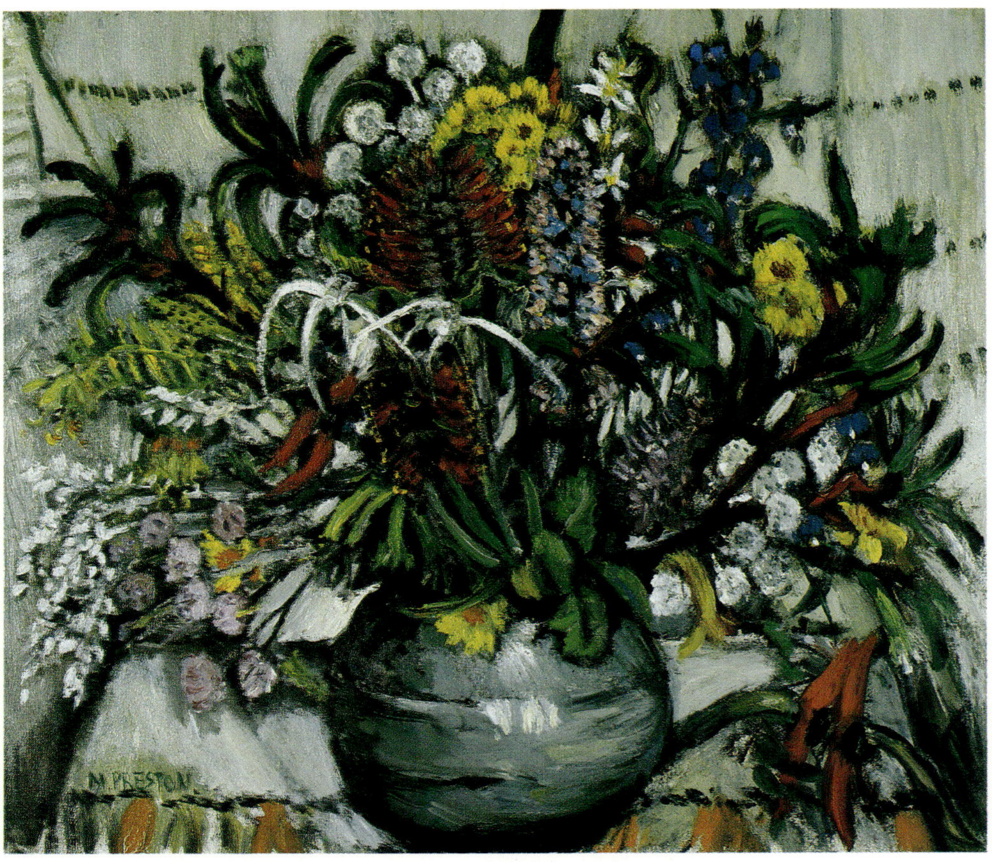

MARGARET PRESTON was Australia's foremost woman artist between the two world wars and is regarded as our finest still life painter. While most women painters of her day received financial help from their families and were not expected to make a living from their art, Margaret Preston was different. She was one of the first women artists in this country to make a successful career from painting. An important feature of her work is that it always displays a strong Australian quality. She would only paint native flowers and plants, for example, banksias, warratahs and wattle. Her compositions were influenced by Japanese art and are strongly defined. There is also an emphasis on texture.

Native Flowers of Western Australia
Margaret Preston
1875 — 1963 (Australian)
43 x 50.8 cm
Art Gallery of Western Australia, Perth

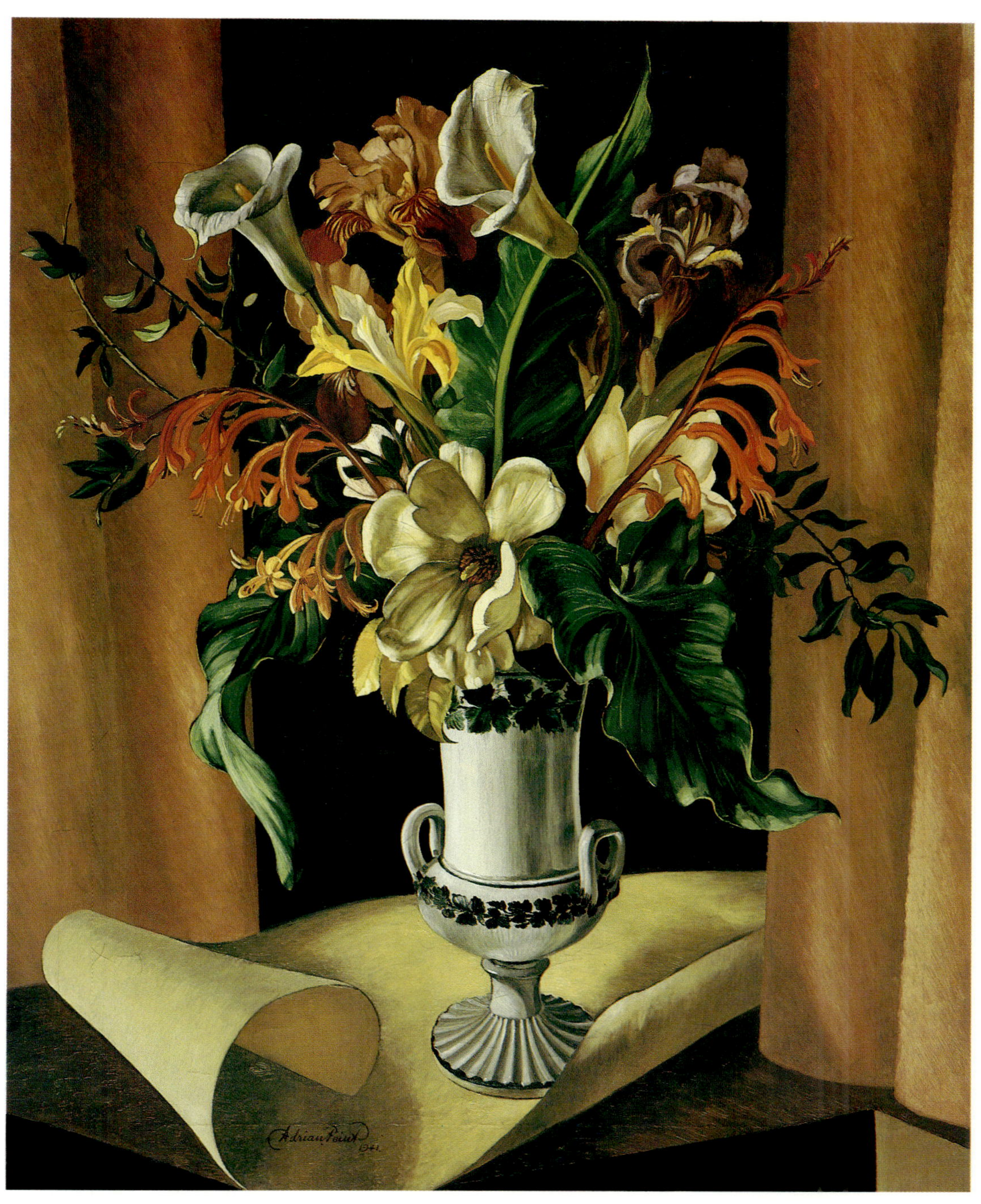

ADRIAN FEINT was another Australian artist who painted still life. His work was more traditional in approach. Unlike Margaret Preston he would often paint exotic flowers, emphasising their formal arrangements. Although the colour in this painting appears flat, Feint introduces a rich colour scheme. The forms are strongly defined and demand our attention. They almost appear as if they are frozen to perfection.

Formal Flower Piece *1941*
Adrian Feint *1894 — 1971 (Australian)*
Oil on canvas
65.8 x 55.6 cm
New England Regional Museum, Armidale

Blue Poles *1952*
Jackson Pollock *1912 — 1956 (American)*
Oil, enamel, aluminium paint and glass on canvas
212 x 489 cm
Australian National Gallery, Canberra

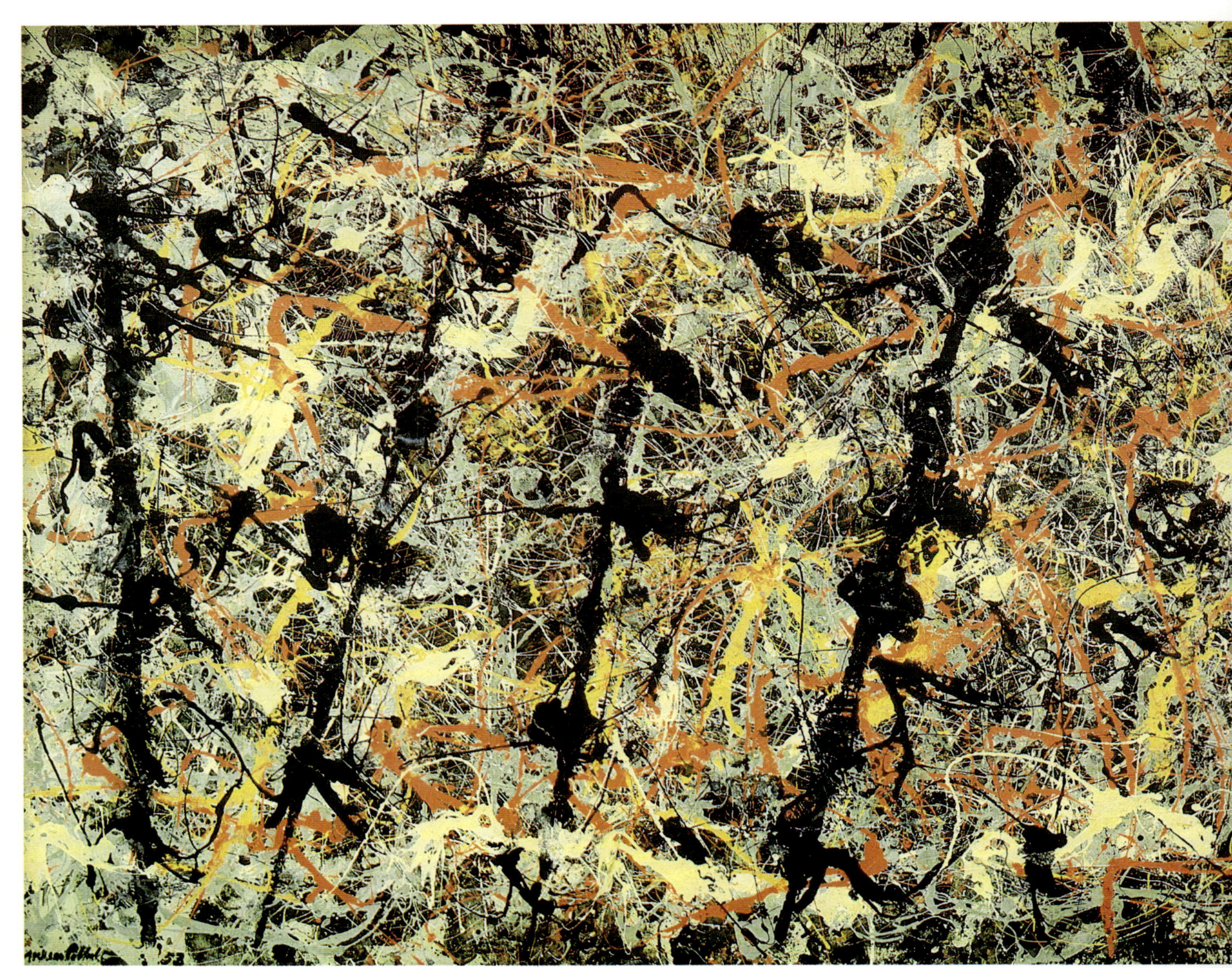

What does the term abstract art really mean? We use it to describe drawn, painted or sculpted images which do not have any obvious meaning or represent anything that we are familiar with. But we can all paint what we feel and it doesn't have to describe places, objects, people or animals. In many ways abstract art is like music. It can be bold, soft, loud, emotional or controlled. Abstract art is a personal language which reveals the imagination of an artist. Although many people comment that anyone can do an abstract painting, the question is always whether it is good or bad and whether the artist's output is consistent. Good art always implies consistency of effort. It is never a one-off exercise. You might, for instance, be able to take a good photograph but to keep on producing to the same standard requires skill and a great deal of knowledge. The abstract painters who have distinguished themselves have all broken new ground. They have created their own unique approach to painting by inventing styles that always clearly bear their signature.

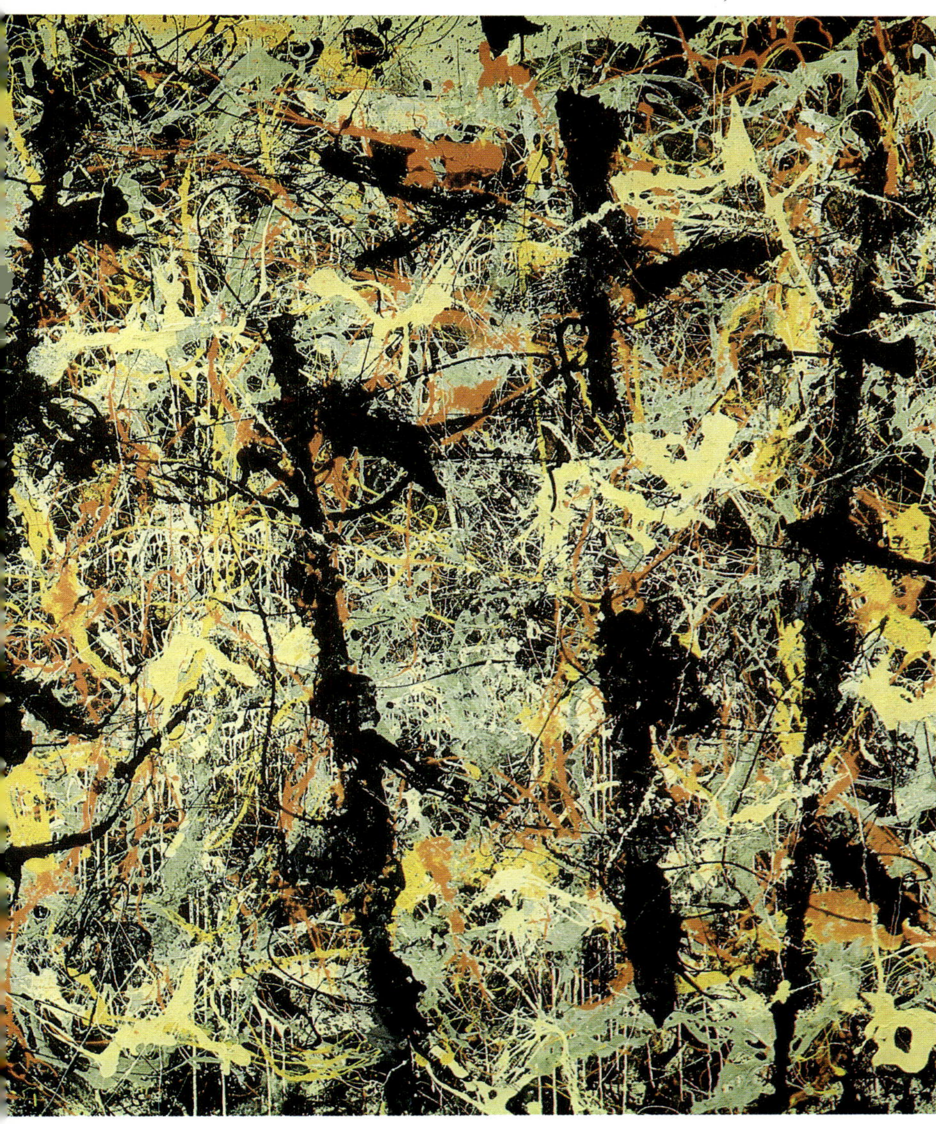

JACKSON POLLOCK was an American artist who painted from the 1930s to the 50s. He was a member of a group of painters who became known as the New York School. All these artists developed their own styles, but their expressive, free approach to painting, known as Abstract Expressionism, influenced artists around the world. *Blue Poles* is regarded as one of Pollock's most important works. The canvas is built up in layers of paint, flung at a distance from the artist's brushes. Pollock produced this painting in a frenzy of activity and added glass and sand to give the canvas a rich texture. *Blue Poles* created a great deal of discussion when the Australian National Gallery purchased it in the early 1970s. It still does, but for a very different reason. Apart from the price paid for the work it created international interest in American abstract art.

TONY TUCKSON was influenced by Abstract Expressionism. He, along with many Australian painters who came back from the Second World War, adopted styles that were becoming popular in the United States and Europe. Tuckson's approach to painting is bold. He almost attacks his canvas and paints it in a matter of seconds using large brush strokes and strong colours.

The painting has a strong emotional impact. Thick solid black forms are splashed against a white background, and hints of red paint fade through the surface. The artist adds to the tension by imposing five bold white lines on the surface which contain the explosive energy of the composition.

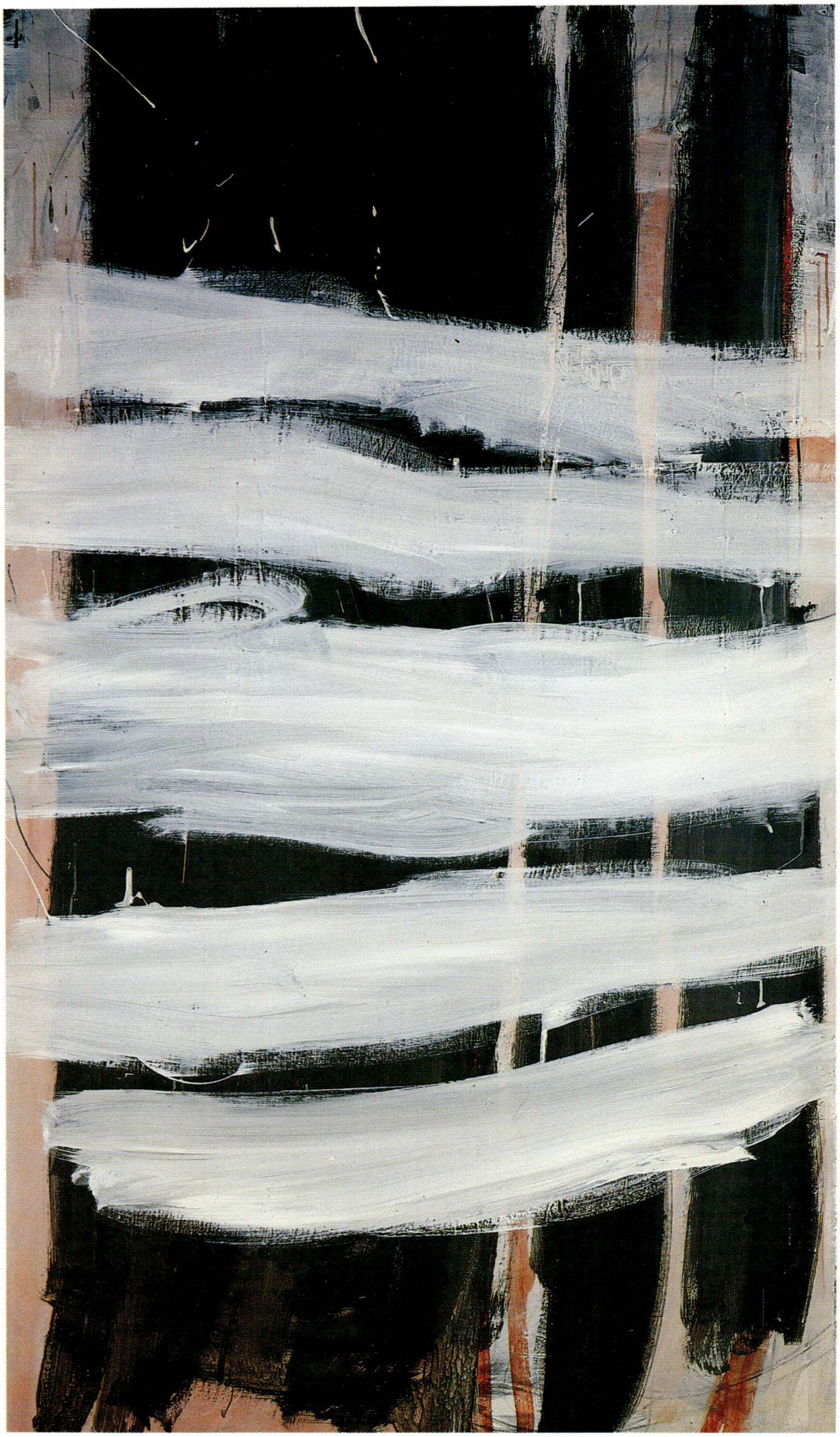

White Lines (horizontal) on Black and Pink *1973*
Tony Tuckson *1921 — 1973 (Australian)*
Synthetic polymer paint on hardboard
214 x 122.5 cm
Art Gallery of South Australia, Adelaide

BY PLACING different colours and shapes together our eyes will sometimes play tricks. For instance, forms and objects will appear to move when they are actually stationary. This is known as the science of optics. In the 1960s many artists and designers were fascinated by optical effects. Bridget Riley is an English painter who became the main exponent of the Op Art movement. In this painting she uses wavy lines and a variety of pastel colours to achieve movement on the canvas.

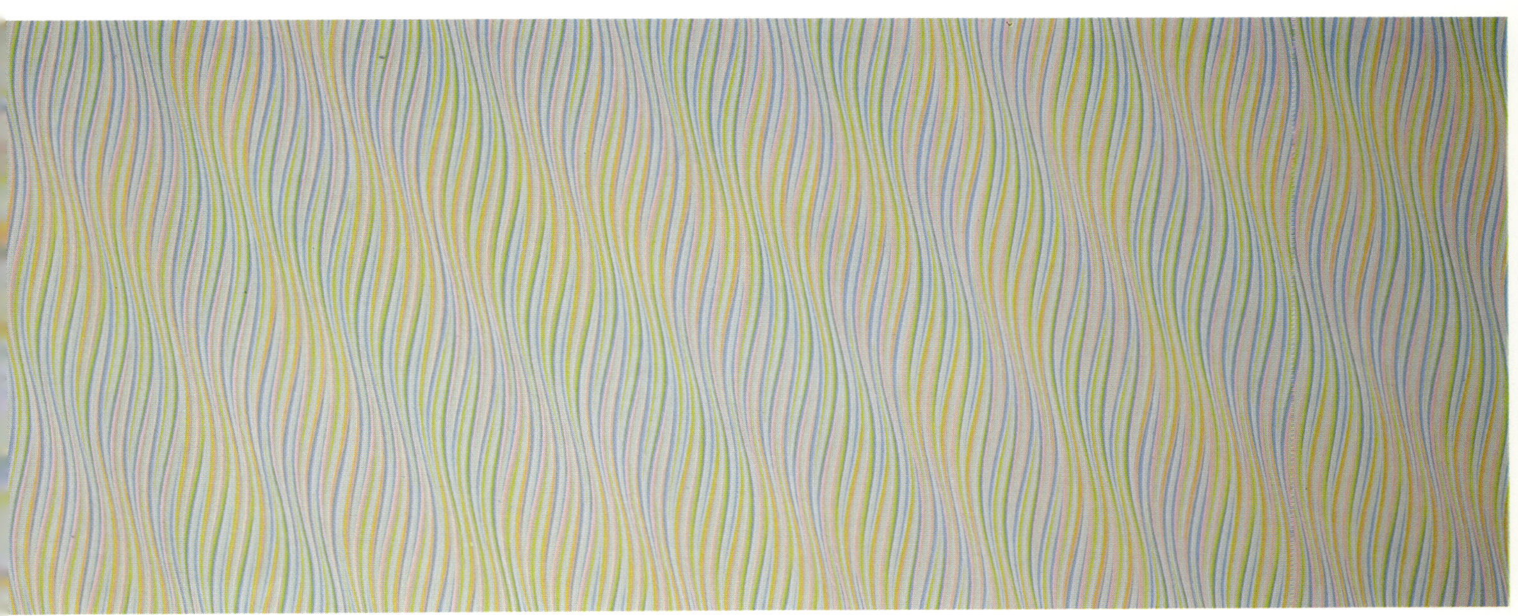

Aurum *1976*
Bridget Riley *b 1931 (English)*
Acrylic on linen
105.5 x 272 cm
Art Gallery of New South Wales, Sydney

Art was always an important part of Aboriginal culture. It still is. Stories about the world, its creation and the plants, animals and various tribes that lived on the Australian continent were developed into myths and legends known as the Dreamtime. Passed down from the tribal elders to the young in painted or spoken form, the Dreamtime stories were also used to convey messages. Aborigines painted on the walls of caves, the bark of trees and even made sand pictures out of different coloured soils. Simple figures were painted with crude brushes or paint was blown from the mouth. Images were either flat shapes of colour with very elaborately patterned backgrounds or painted in x-ray style, so that you can see their bones and insides. Paint was made from natural colour pigments that came from vegetation and various soils, mixed with the sticky juice of lily roots or other natural glues.

ABORIGINAL TRIBES developed many myths and rituals about the annual rainfall. These rituals were particularly important in the dry arid land of Central Australia where food was sometimes scarce. This painting by Johnny Warangula depicts the land before and after a successful rain ceremony. The wavy pink lines represent dry creek beds before they begin to flow again with the rains. The brown and black areas are the roots of plants, collected and eaten by Aboriginal tribes. The circles represent small pockets of water that collect underground. Also depicted are striped circles which represent a species of fungi (like a mushroom) which grows under the witchetty bushes after the rains. The plain circles are the fungi that grow underground.

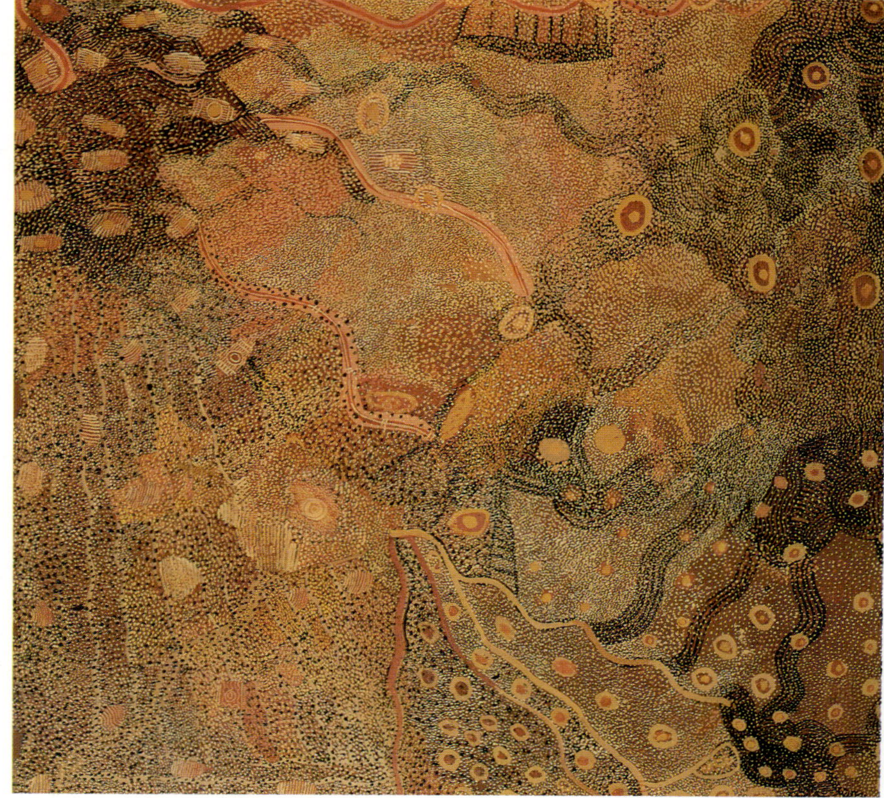

Water Dreaming *1977*
Johnny Warangula Tjupurrula *(Australian Aboriginal)*
Bark Painting
45 x 62 cm
Northern Territory Museum of Arts and Sciences, Darwin

MANY ABORIGINAL artists maintain the traditions of their ancestors. This bark painting by Lofty Nabarrayal, depicts a cat fish. The x-ray style was used by many Aboriginal tribes in Australia.

Spoonbill and Fish *c. 1970*
Lofty Nabarrayal Nadjamerrek *b 1926 (Australian Aboriginal)*
Bark Painting
Northern Territory Museum of Arts and Sciences, Darwin

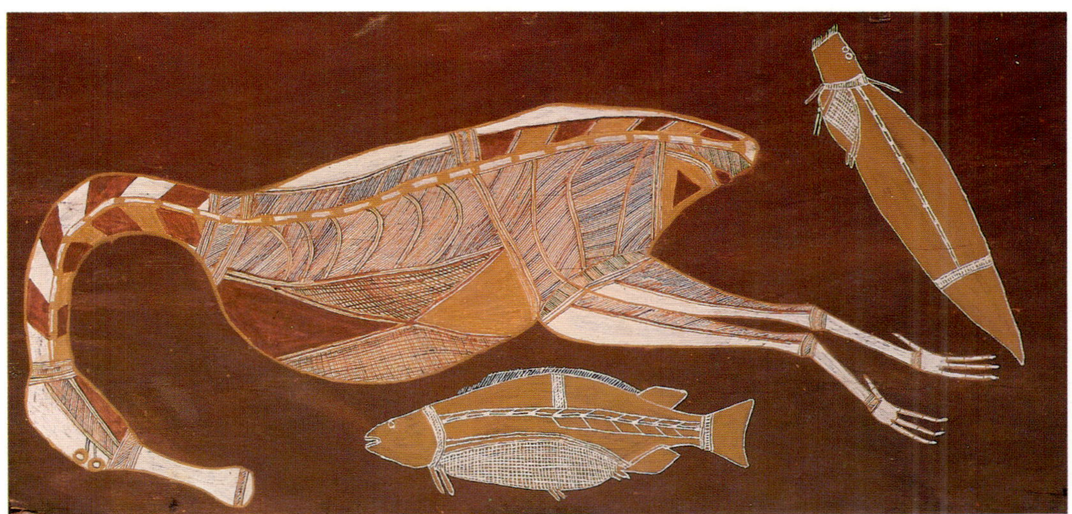

FOR THOUSANDS of years Aboriginal tribes painted and carved on the wall of caves. These caves were sacred sites and depicted stories about the Dreamtime. This is a detail of a cave painting which shows a Supreme Deity called Timara who is the guardian to the entrance of Woolunda, the resting place in preparation for life after death. The thin three-metre high figure in dark red is an Aboriginal ancestor who hovers above. He is turning one leg upward. This was part of a ritual known as the dingo ceremony dance. The figure is miming a dingo marking its territory.

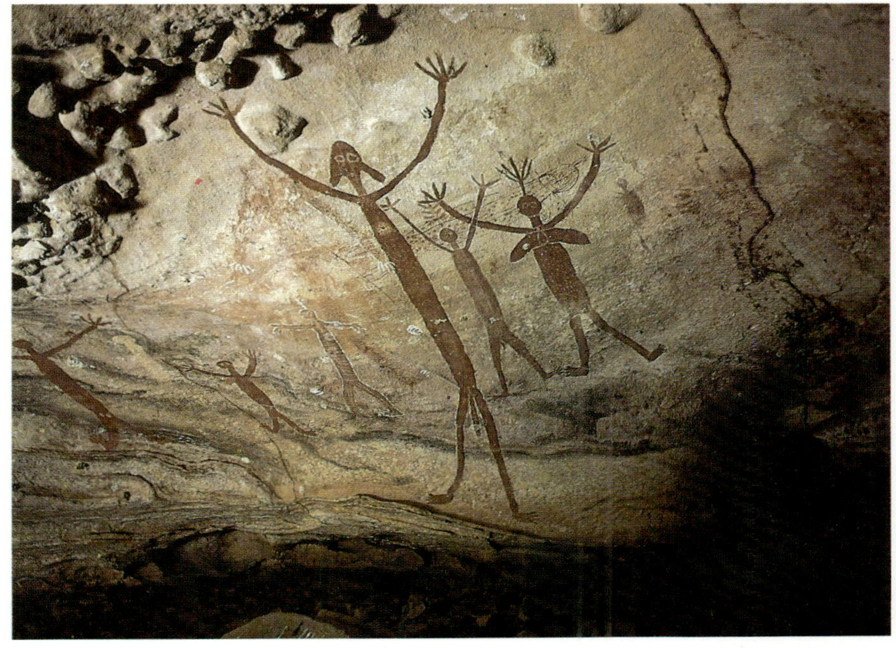

Cave Painting *c. 14,000 BC*
Aboriginal Origins
Quinkin Cave, Northern Queensland

Artists are sometimes like journalists. They often record events and moments in time which reflect what has happened, what people are doing and how they react to life. Coverage of politics and social behaviour or events is not necessarily restricted to newspapers or current affairs programmes. Throughout history artists have been employed to paint records of events such as victorious battles, remarkable voyages and the discovery of new lands. They would often accompany armies on campaigns and were considered important members of scientific teams. We can learn a lot about a society's social attitudes, beliefs, politics even its achievements by simply looking at an artist's interpretation of the world.

MANY EARLY settlers sat for family portraits. These paintings tell us a lot about our pioneers, the way they lived and their social position. One Melbourne family that became important was the O'Mullane family. This is a group portrait of Maria Elizabeth O'Mullane and her children which was painted by an unknown artist in 1851. The painting shows that the O'Mullanes had become very prosperous. They are wearing fine clothes no doubt imported from England. Their sitting room also features in the portrait, and reveals that the family lived in a pleasant, middle-class environment.

Mrs O'Mullane met her husband on the ship out to Australia in 1839. He was a doctor who became a wealthy and respected man in the colony. The family lived in Queen Street and later Bourke Street in the early days when Melbourne was a small colonial town. Dr O'Mullane named two streets that today are well known — Grattan Street in Carlton and Grenville Street in Prahran.

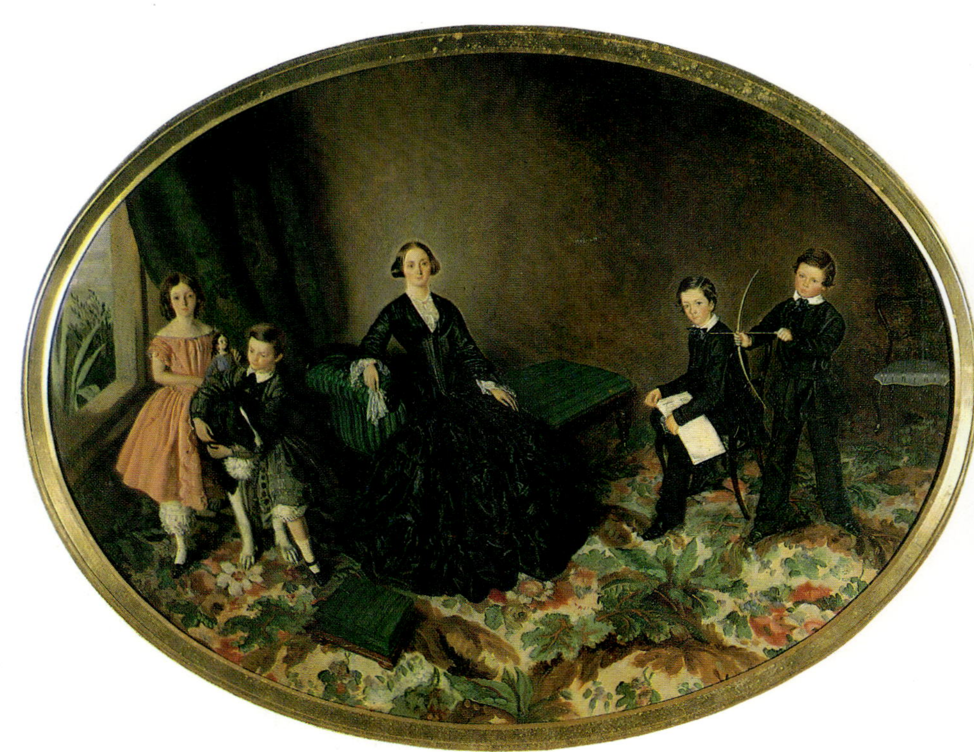

Maria Elizabeth O'Mullane and her children *c. 1850*
Anon
Oil on canvas
57.8 x 90.2 cm
National Gallery of Victoria, Melbourne

WHILE SOME settlers became wealthy and successful others found life very difficult. When Frederick McCubbin painted *Down on his Luck* in 1889, many pioneers had problems making a living from the land. This painting shows an unknown settler faced with an uncertain future.

Down on his Luck was painted well after the gold rush days of the 1850s. The success of the gold fields of Victoria encouraged many new migrants to try and make their fortunes from prospecting. But for the majority the land was not paved with gold. Many became sad figures of rural poverty. In this painting McCubbin portrays an unsuccessful gold digger. The figure, painted from a model who posed in the open air, sits at a fire. His hand is raised to his forehead. The grey dusk of the landscape also reflects his sombre mood.

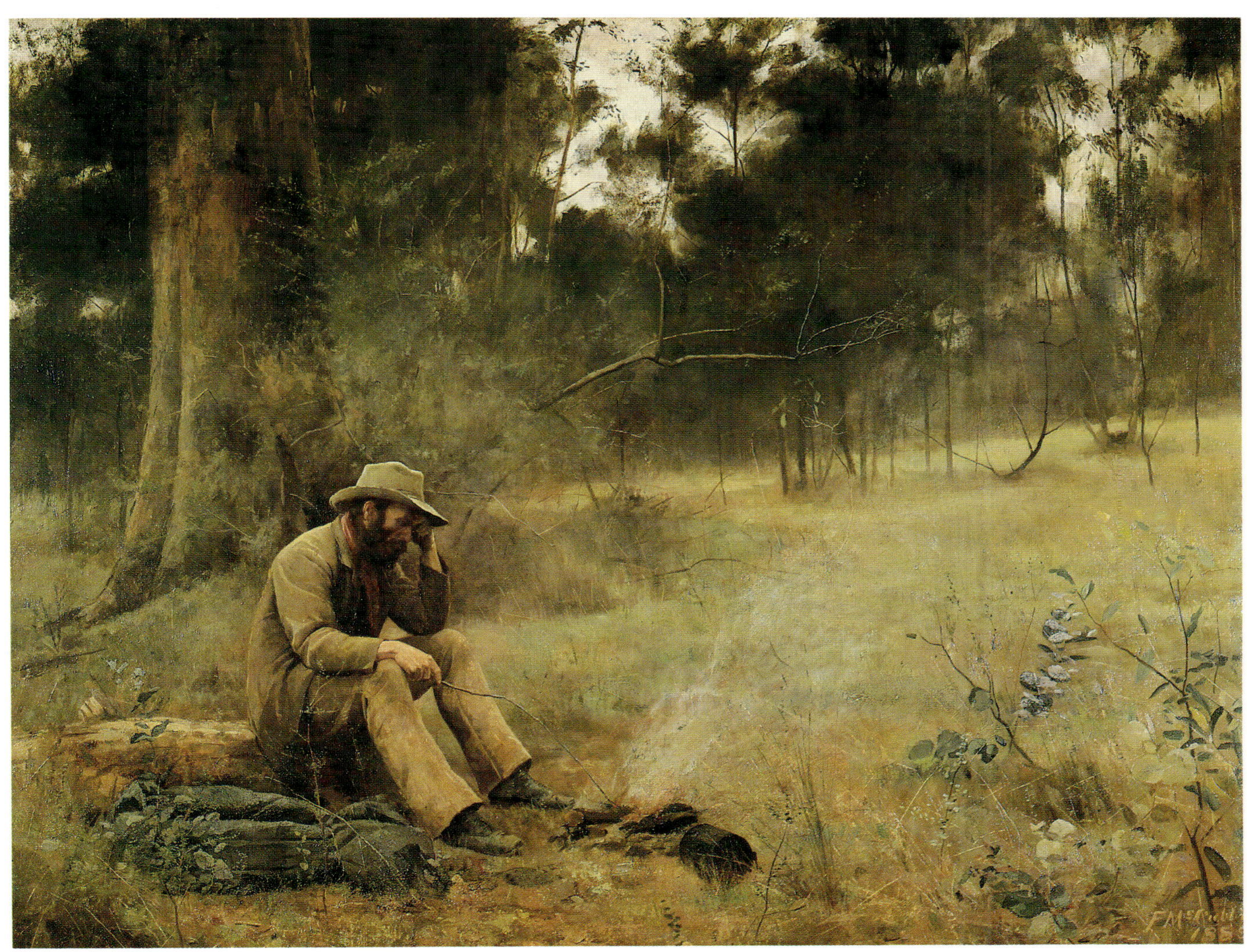

Down on his Luck *1889*
Frederick McCubbin *1855 — 1917 (Australian)*
Oil on canvas
112.5 x 150 cm
Art Gallery of Western Australia, Perth

RUSSELL DRYSDALE painted many scenes of the Australian outback. But his favourite subjects were the people who survived its loneliness. Drysdale often portrayed the women of the outback as people of great strength who had adjusted to the harshness of the land. In *Woman in a Landscape*, painted in 1949, Drysdale pays tribute to the pioneering women of the Australian outback — the women who ran the stations while their husbands spent months away from their families rounding up cattle.

The woman dominates the painting, dwarfing the buildings in the background. Her monumental scale juts out of the foreground and is as solid as a block of granite. But the background reveals the vastness of the Australian outback. The glowing red plains which seem to go on forever are broken by the horizon. A golden blue haze of an evening sky settles over the plains. Drysdale paints a landscape that is as eerie and as desolate as the moon itself.

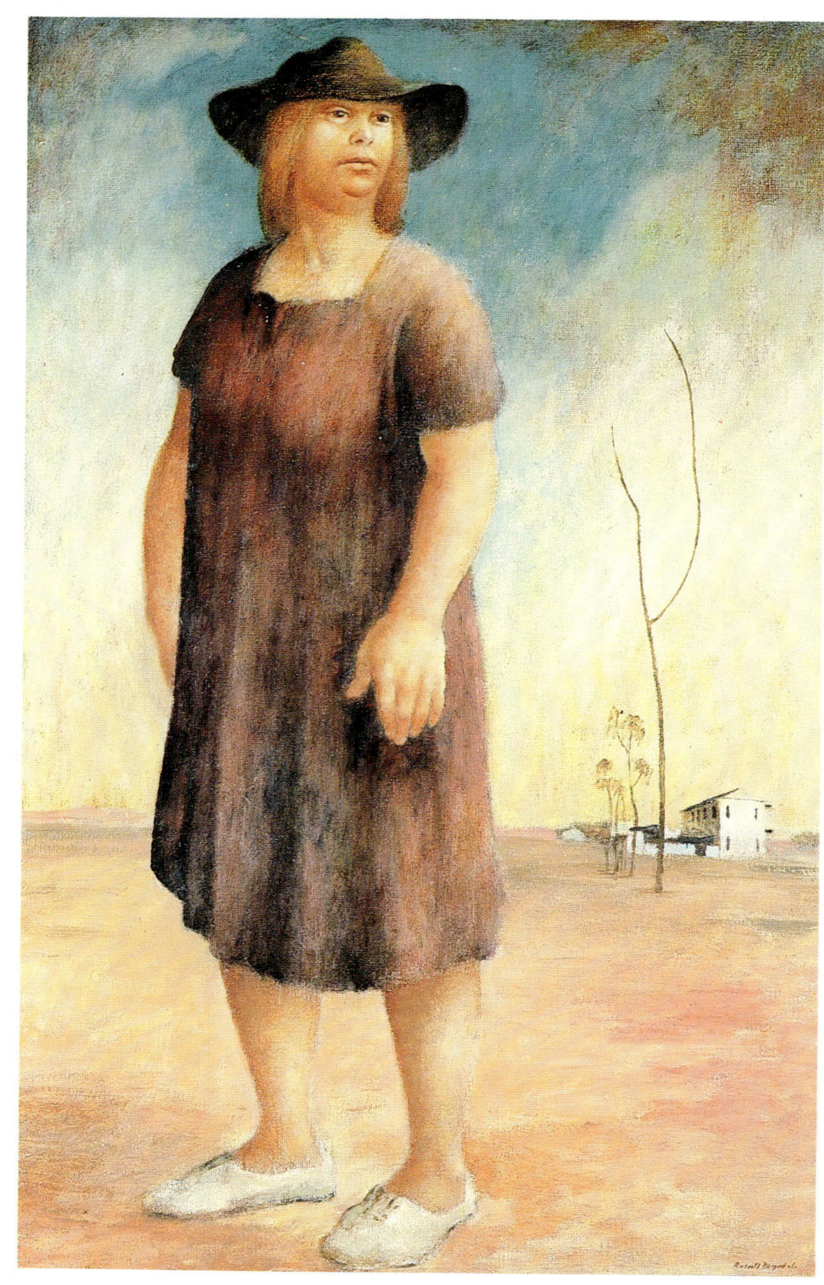

Woman in a Landscape *1949*
Sir George Russell Drysdale *1912 — 1981 (Australian)*
Oil on composition board
101 x 66.3 cm
Art Gallery of South Australia, Adelaide

POLITICS WAS important to Peter Purves-Smith. He lived during the time when Hitler's Germany was making war on Europe. *The Nazis, Nuremburg*, painted in 1938, is an important record of what was happening in Europe at the time. This painting was inspired by Germany's invasion of Austria. The flags and the long lines of soldiers and the big cannons pointing out of the picture remind us of the horrors of war.

Purves-Smith tells us what he thinks about the Nazis by making the soldiers look a bit foolish, they are portrayed as paper dolls or marionettes, arranged in diagonal lines and marching to the goose step. Their arms are either absurdly elongated as they salute or they stand mindlessly erect, holding bayonets.

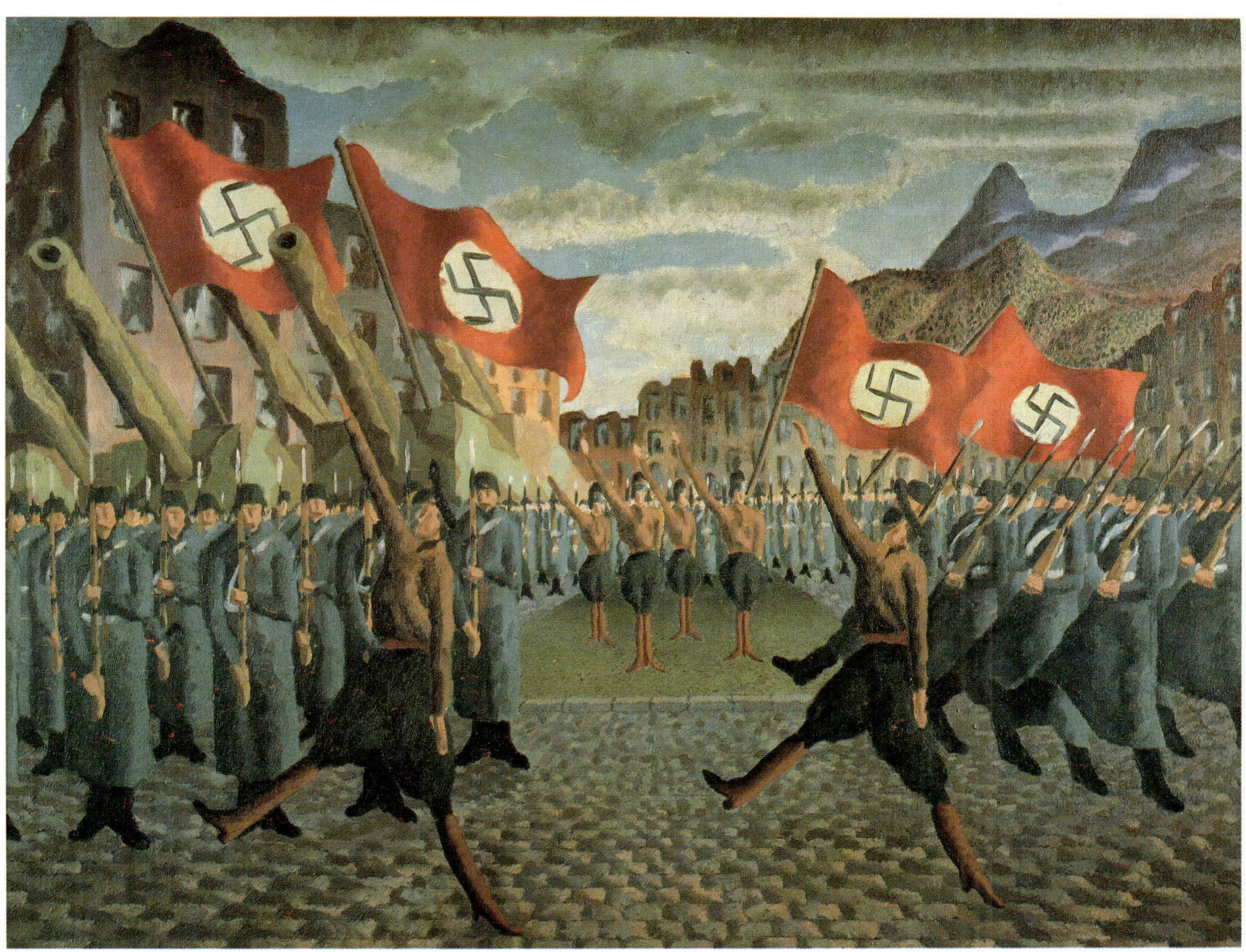

The Nazis, Nuremburg, *1938*
Peter Purves-Smith *1912 — 1949 (Australian)*
Oil on canvas
71.4 x 91.4 cm
Queensland Art Gallery, Brisbane

NED KELLY is the most famous of all our bushrangers and therefore a special figure in Australian folklore. He is often portrayed as the victim of injustice, someone who was prepared to fight for the rights of the individual. He is the favourite subject of Sidney Nolan, one of Australia's most respected painters.

In this painting Sidney Nolan depicts the final event that led up to the capture of the Kelly Gang whose members were sent to prison to be hanged. Wearing a large black metal mask and protective armour, Ned Kelly dominates the scene. He and his gang have been forced out of the pub at Glenrowan which has been set on fire. Kelly, surrounded by police, is portrayed as a hero determined to fight to the last. Even though Sidney Nolan was re-telling a well-known story, he was still free to be inventive. At the battle of Glenrowan there were not as many police as there are in the painting but the artist wants us to believe that this is a major battle. The goat on the left of the painting, for instance, is a regimental mascot. It is very doubtful the police would have taken a mascot with them. The uniforms of the police are also an invention of the artist — the police who hunted down the Kelly gang wore clothes more suited to the bush, but Nolan puts them into blue and gold uniforms and helmets to make them more recognisable.

Every country has its own stories, myths and legends, which we refer to as folklore. Folklore is the passing down, from generation to generation, of traditional beliefs and customs in story form. While these stories usually deal with events or characters that have been invented, sometimes people who really existed become a symbol for society and a part of popular folklore. Over the years their stories might be exaggerated so they are used to represent attitudes like the triumph of good over evil, the individual rebelling against society, or even to tell a cautionary tale as in many nursery rhymes. Artists often use characters from folklore to explore themes for their art.

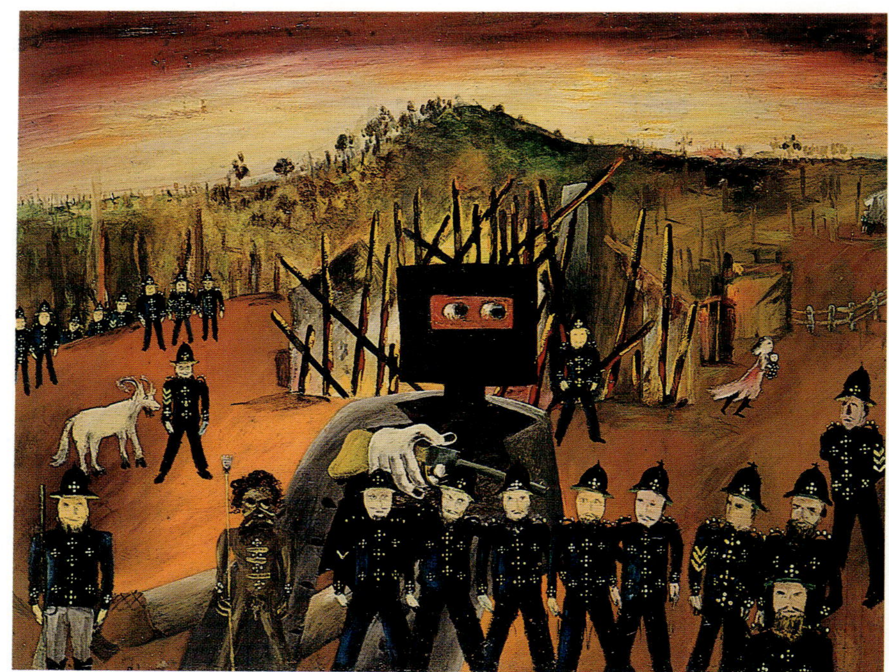

Glenrowan *1946*
Sidney Nolan *b 1917 (Australian)*
Enamel on composition board
91 x 121.5 cm
Australian National Gallery, Canberra

LIKE COWBOYS of the American west, Australian bushrangers have become an important part of our folklore. A popular theme for television and film, bushrangers have also been the subject of many novels and numerous paintings.

Tom Roberts is considered one of our most important painters. He began painting towards the end of the 19th century. With several other well-known artists he formed the Heidelberg School (named after a suburb of Melbourne). They all painted landscapes in the open air. They believed that the most important thing an artist should look for when painting a landscape was the first impression of colour.

Roberts was fascinated by the Australian bush. *Bailed Up* is one of his best-known works. It was painted over a very long period of time from 1895 to 1927, long after the last bushranger was captured. This painting gives a realistic description of what it would have been like to be robbed by outlaws. The landscape, the horse-drawn carriage and the people are very life-like.

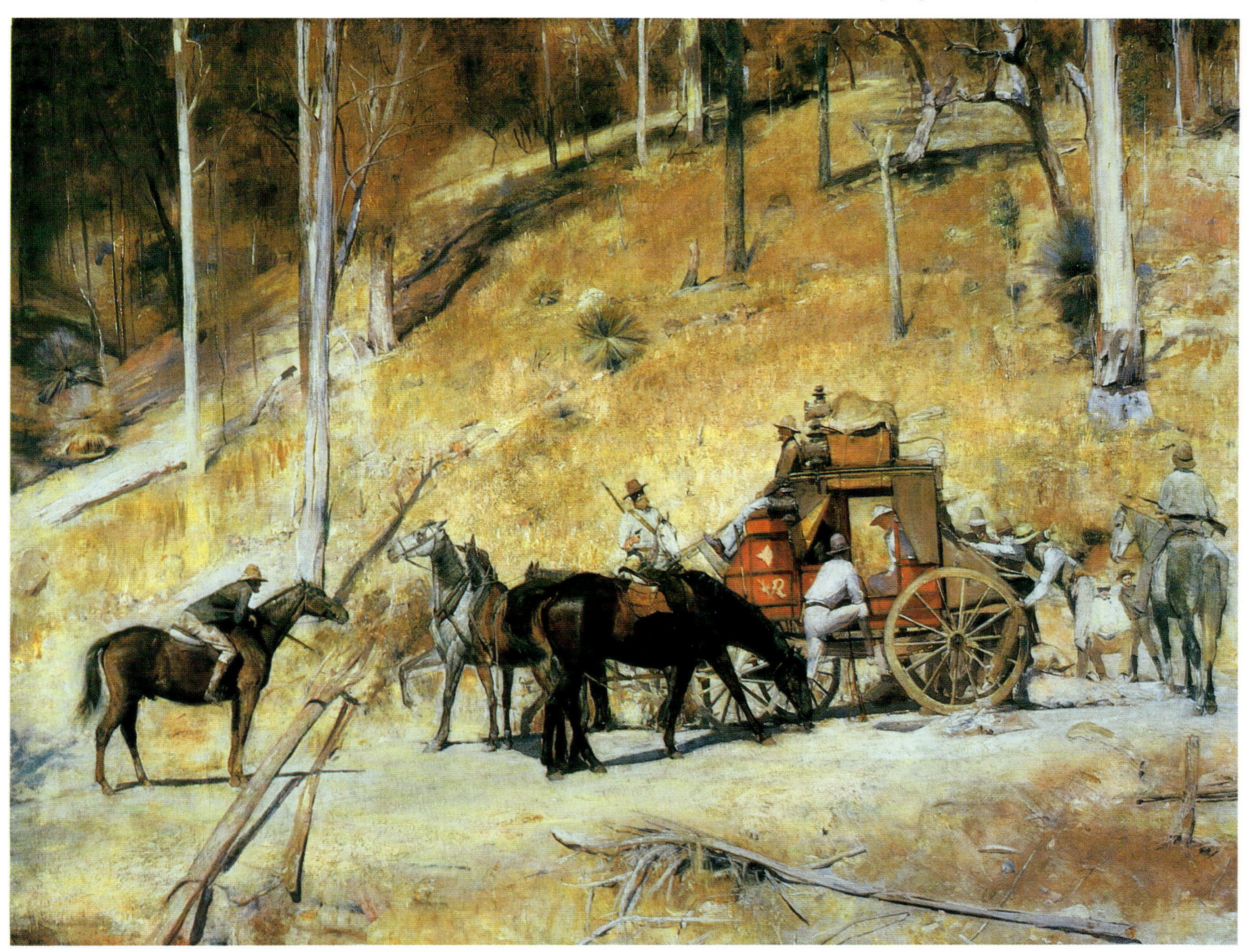

Bailed Up *1895 — 1927*
Tom Roberts *1856 — 1931 (English/Australian)*
Oil on canvas
134.5 x 182.8 cm
Art Gallery of New South Wales

THE LANGUAGE OF ART

Painting, like language is a means of communication – a way of expressing moods, stories, imagined events and feelings. As with any language, in order to understand it you have to learn the vocabulary.

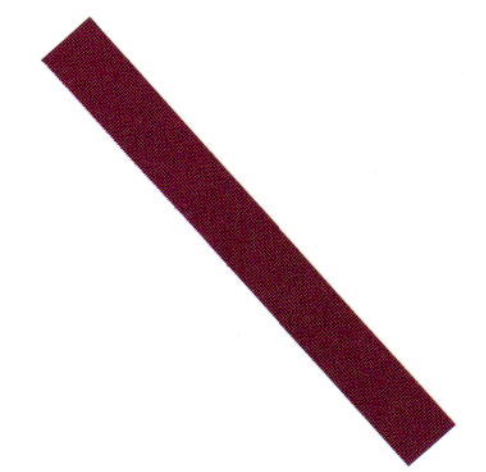

THE STARTING POINT — ASSOCIATIONS

When we see bright colours, like reds, yellows, blues, pinks and greens, we usually think of happy things such as flowers or a circus. Seeing one thing and thinking or feeling another is called 'association'. It is through the use of association that artists can create mood. Associations don't just work for colours. For instance, a smooth wavy line might make us think of the sea, or a pleasant dream. A jagged line could make us think of mountains, of lightning or anger.

THE SUBJECT MATTER

In a painting that represents something that we can recognise — representational painting — this 'language' is used to 'talk about' the particular subject matter, but in an abstract painting, the language itself becomes the subject matter. Knowing the 'language' can help us enjoy looking at paintings because we can understand them better, and appreciate what the artist was aiming for.

SCALE

Perhaps the first thing you will notice about a painting is how big it is. Whilst sheer size in itself can be impressive, it doesn't necessarily follow that because it's big it's good. There are some delightful miniature paintings which are like jewels, as carefully crafted as a cut diamond.

So what influences the artist when it comes to choosing the size of the work? Well for one thing, paintings that were made to hang in homes tend to be smaller than paintings intended for public display in art galleries and public buildings.

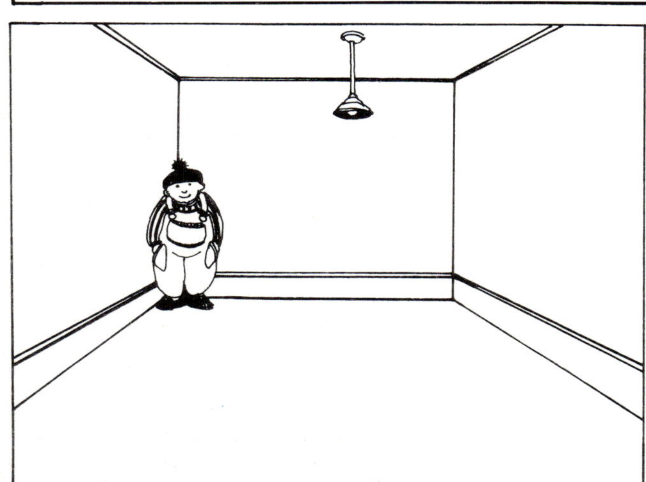

In this picture, the subject of the painting is very small in relation to the amount of background. The room is of more importance than the boy, so we are very aware that the boy is all alone and probably feeling a bit miserable.

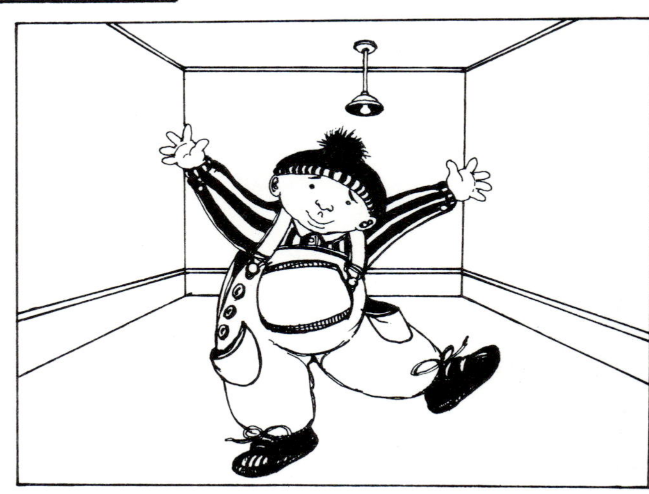

Now look at this painting. The boy leaps up right in front of our eyes — the room itself becomes a minor detail, all our attention is focused on the boy and it gives us quite a different feeling. Look again at the painting by Russell Drysdale on page 28.

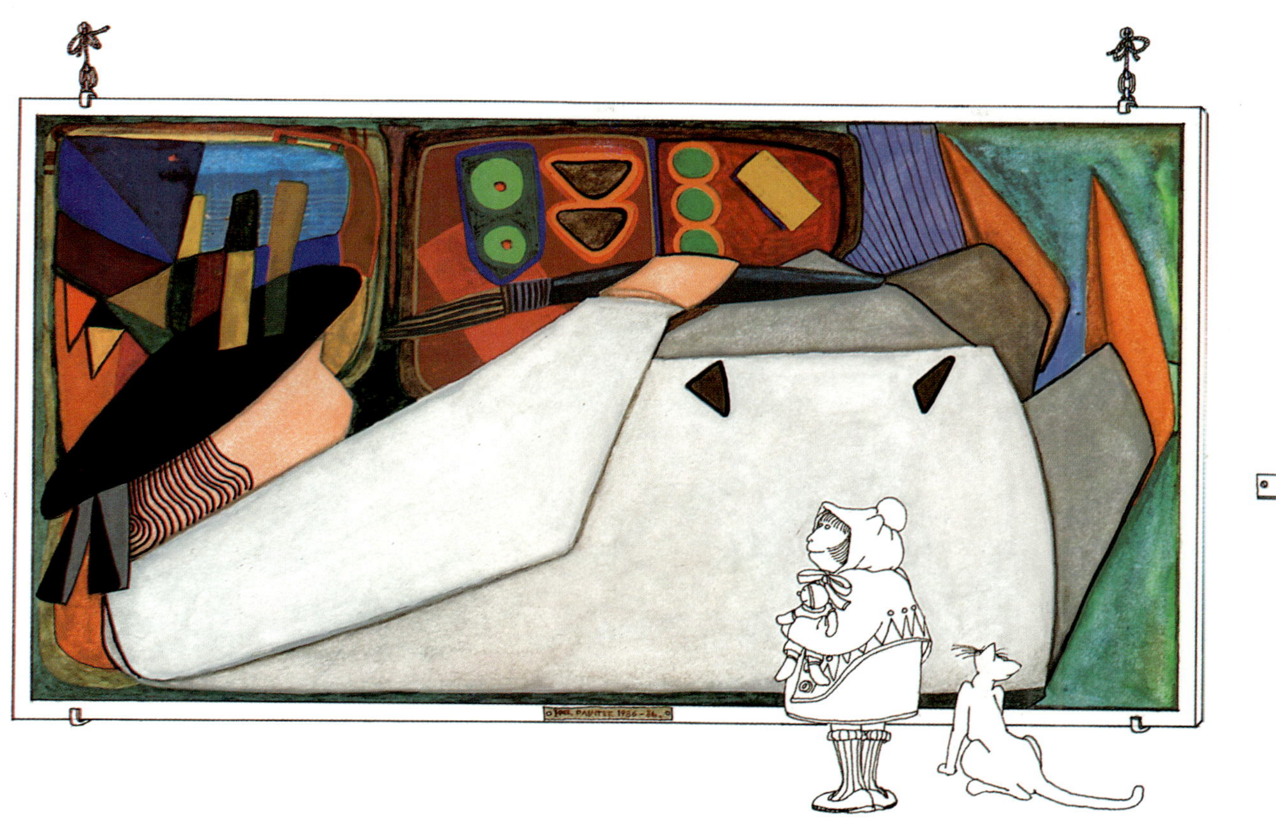

Paintings that are made to be hung in public galleries are quite often much larger...

SPACE

A small child in a large, empty room will seem lonely and sad. A big person sitting on a very small chair will look rather funny. A lot of people in a telephone booth will look very crowded. This 'relationship of size' — the size of something compared with its surroundings — is another part of the artist's language. It can communicate mood.

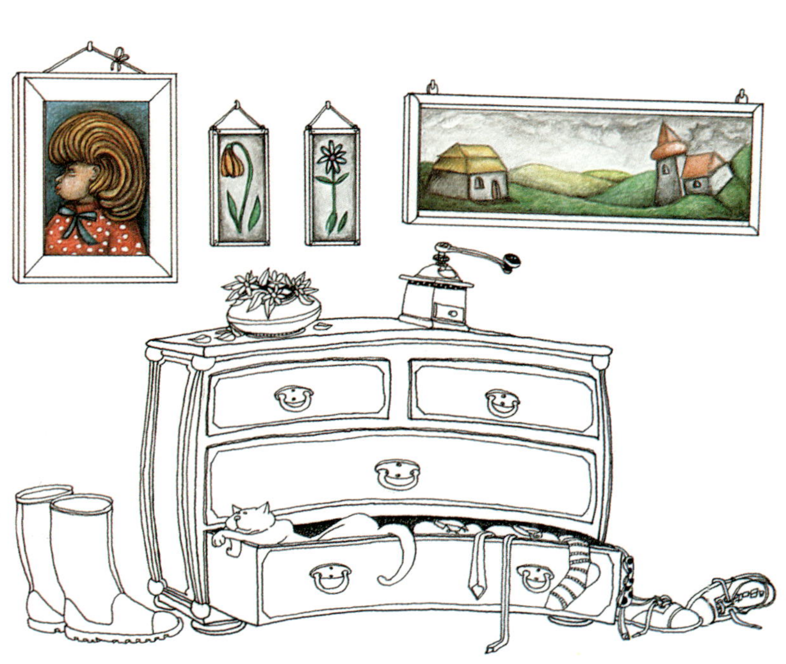

...than paintings intended for homes.

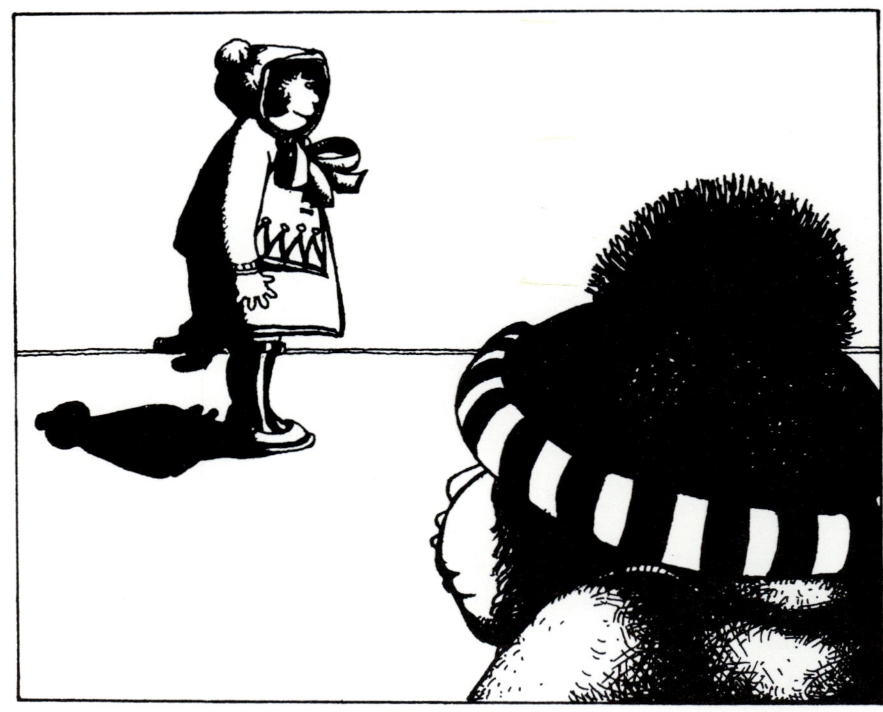

CHEATING THE EYE —THE RULES OF PERSPECTIVE

Things look much bigger to us when they are close up than when they are a long way away. If an artist was to paint the back of a person's head very big on one side of the picture and on the other side a full-length person only the height of the head, you would not see it as an enormous head with a very small person standing beside it, you would see a person very close to you and a person far away. This illusion of near and far was discovered by the ancient Greeks, and re-discovered in Florence, Italy about 500 years ago. It is called 'perspective'. The successful use of perspective will make you forget you are looking at a flat, two-dimensional painting and give you the feeling that you could walk into it and explore.

Perspective of scale
What can you see? A boy standing close to you and looking at a girl in the distance, or the back of a boy's head and a midget?

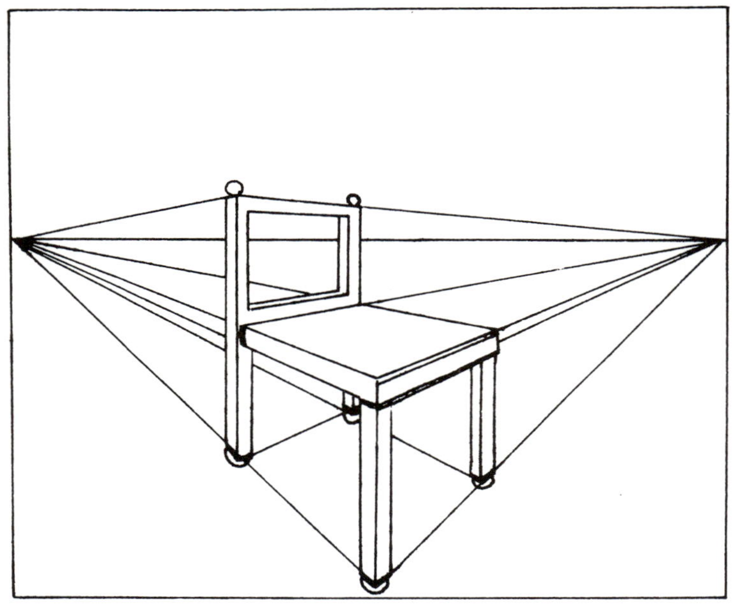

Linear perspective
Here's a chair that really looks as if you could sit on it. Count how many 'vanishing points' there are.

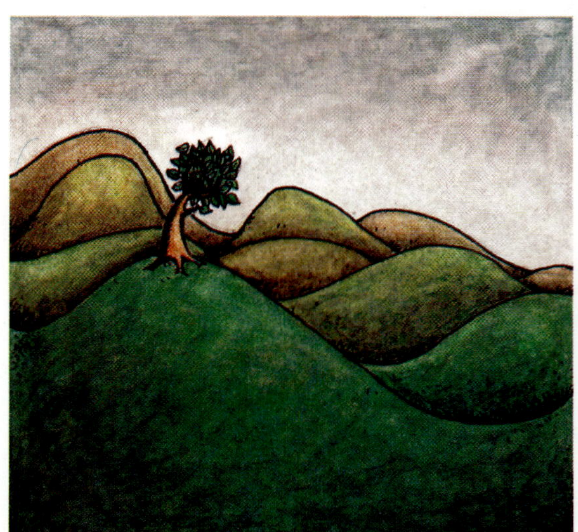

Perspective of colour
Objects lose their colour before they lose their shape.

Linear perspective

Classic perspective relies on the use of a 'vanishing point' which is a point on the horizon (either in or out of the picture) at which all the straight lines going in the same direction meet. Most pictures using linear perspective will have more than one vanishing point.

Perspective of scale:

Needless to say, objects that are nearer appear larger than similar objects that are further away. So the painter makes the objects in front — in the 'foreground' bigger than the rest.

By organising a painting into three distinct areas — a 'foreground', a 'middleground' and a 'background', the painter can create a great feeling of distance.

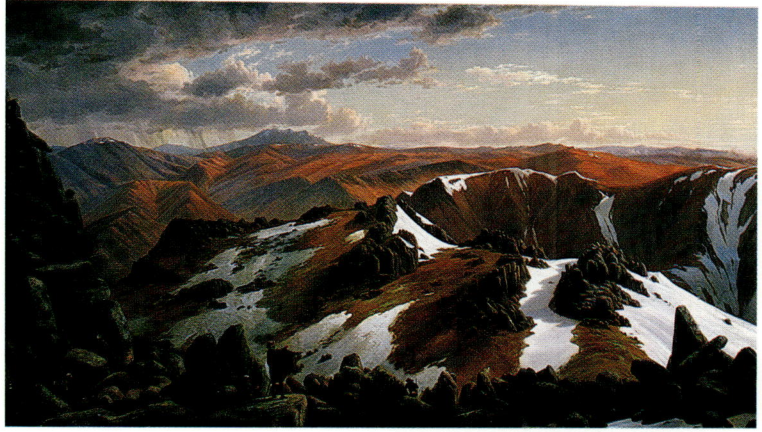

Perspective of colour — or aerial perspective

A red object close to you will seem redder than the same object far away. This is because distant objects lose their colour before they lose their shape, so the feeling of distance is often reinforced by using a lighter colour.

Foreground, middleground and background

Look again at the picture by Eugen von Guerard. Now look at the way the picture has been divided into three distinct areas to give a feeling of depth and distance.

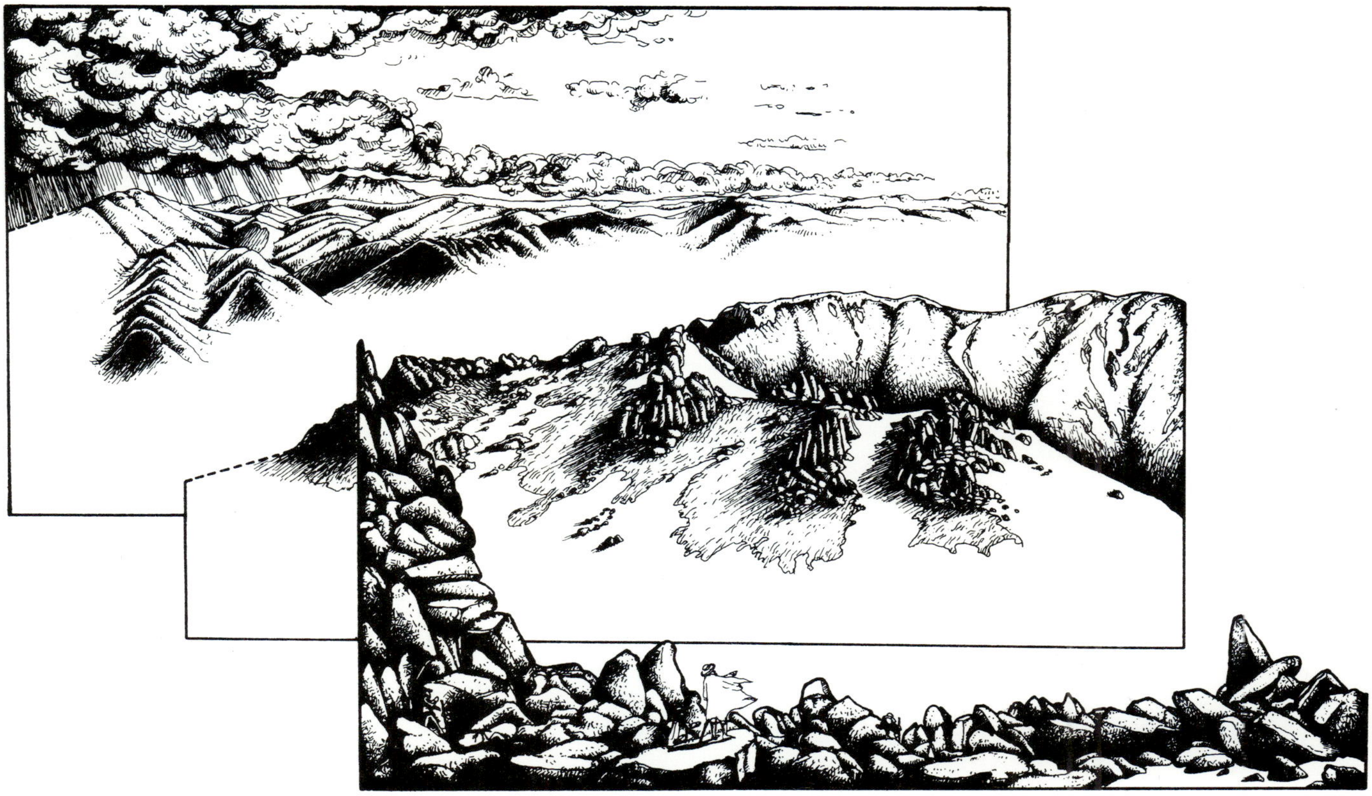

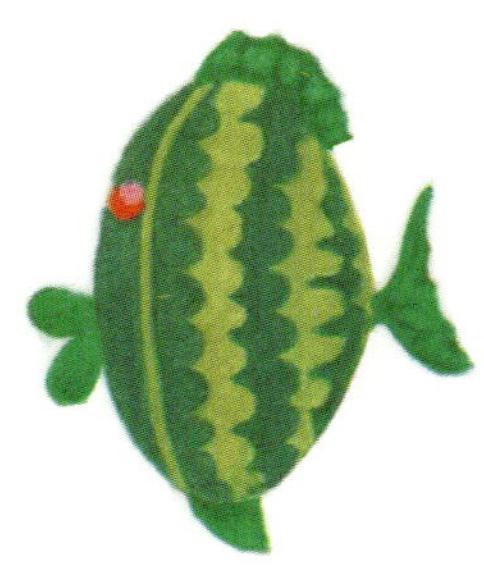

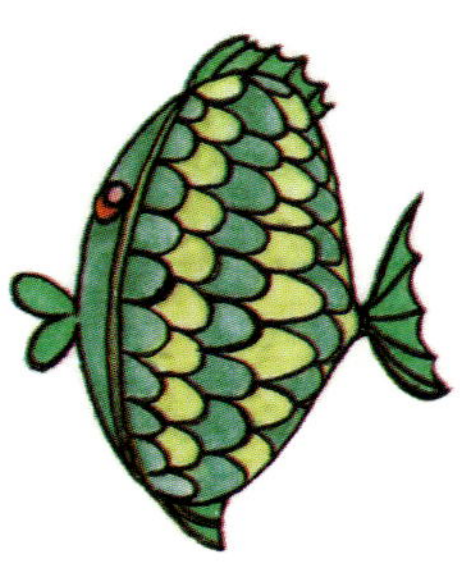

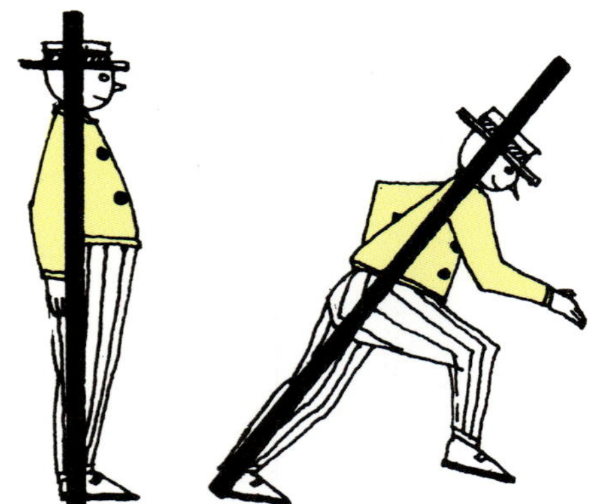

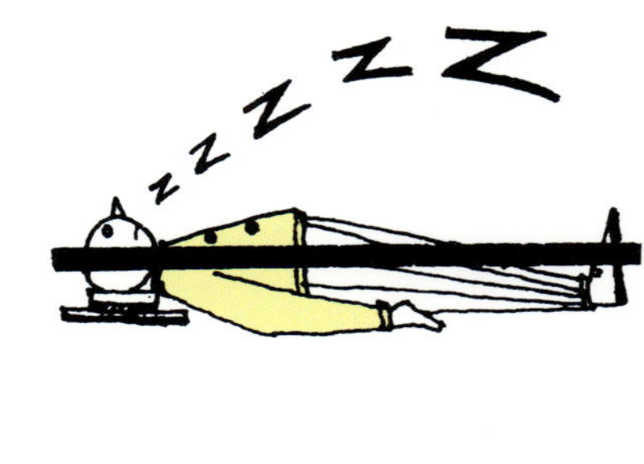

LINE

You will notice that in some paintings, the forms, or shapes appear to have outlines, while in others the shapes appear to grow out of the background.

Lines themselves have a language. For instance a straight line makes the eye want to travel along with it. Simple curves and waves also make the eye want to follow. But once a shape gets too complicated, the eye wanders off. It is precisely because the eye follows lines that lines have associations in our minds — vertical lines make us think of being ready for action, standing up, alert and awake. Horizontal lines make us think of lying down, and a diagonal is associated with movement and energy.

The quality of the line also acts on the subconscious — fine thin lines suggest delicacy, spiky lines suggest anxiety, dotted lines suggest uncertainty and so on.

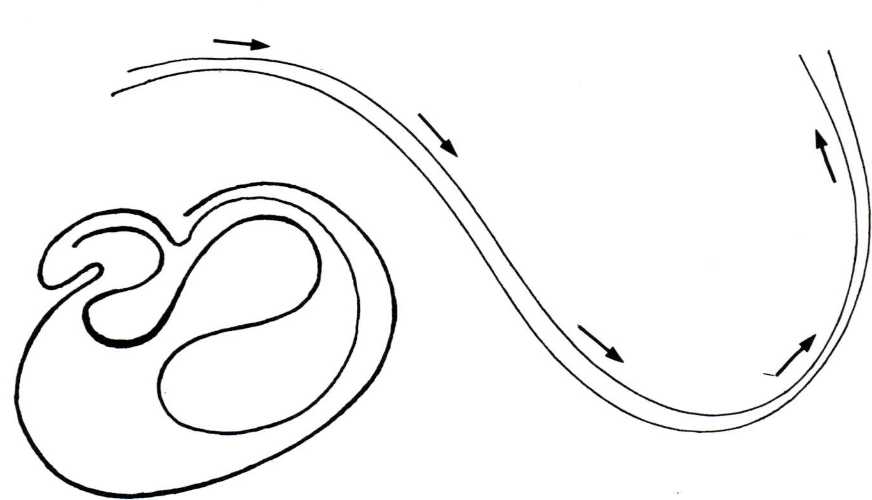

Copy these lines onto a sheet of paper and doodle around them. It's surprising how many different ideas can be suggested by a simple line.▼

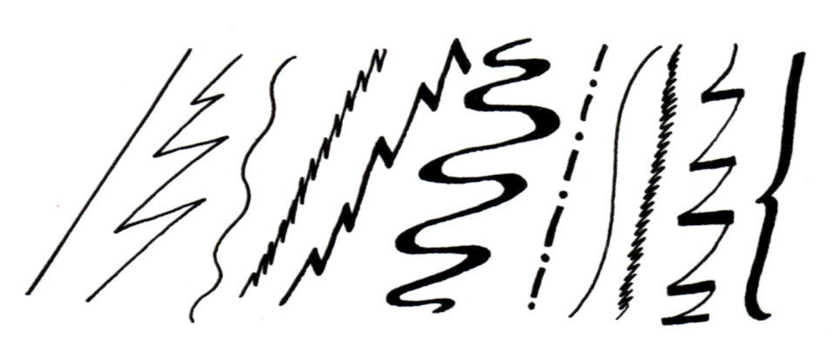

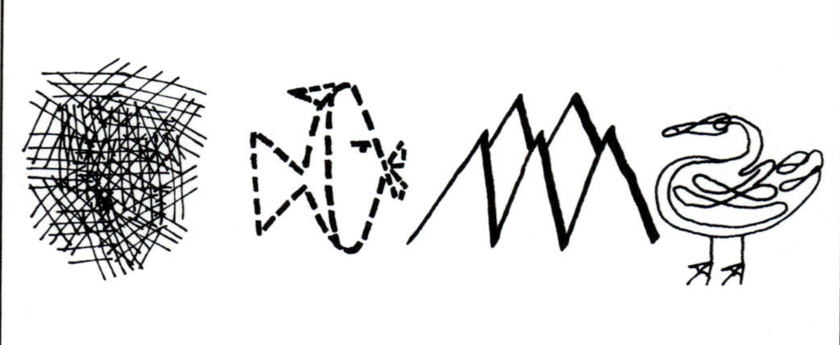

It's the same apple, but in each case the light is coming from a different angle.

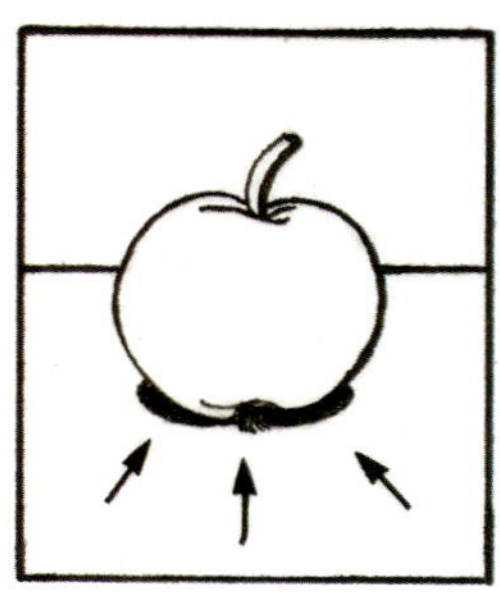 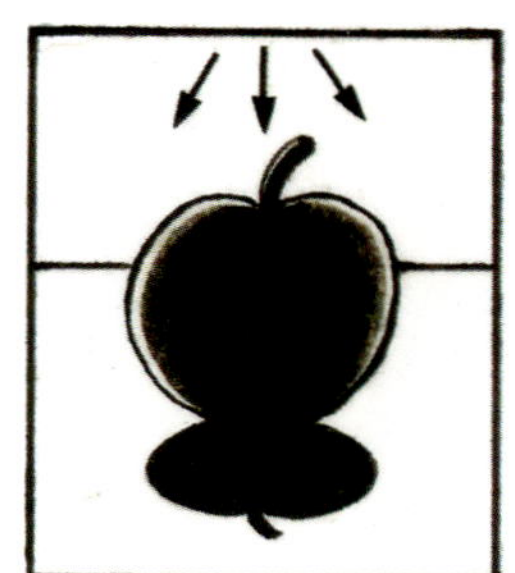 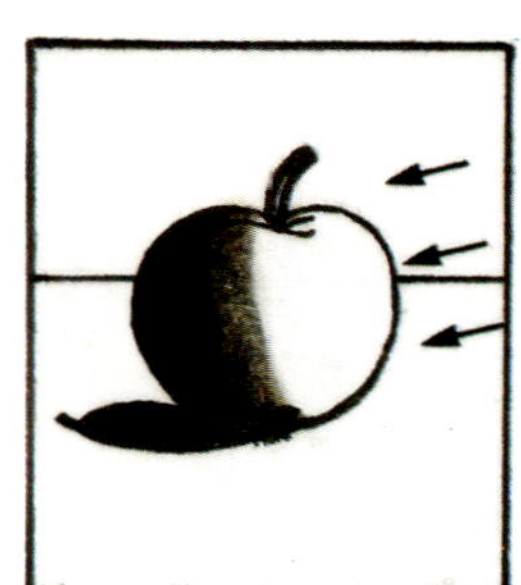

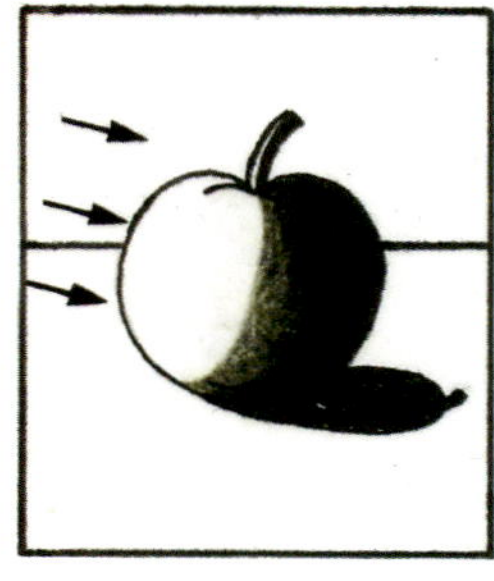 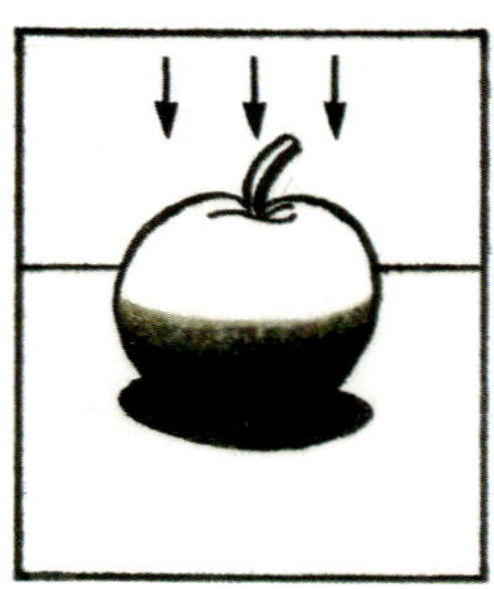 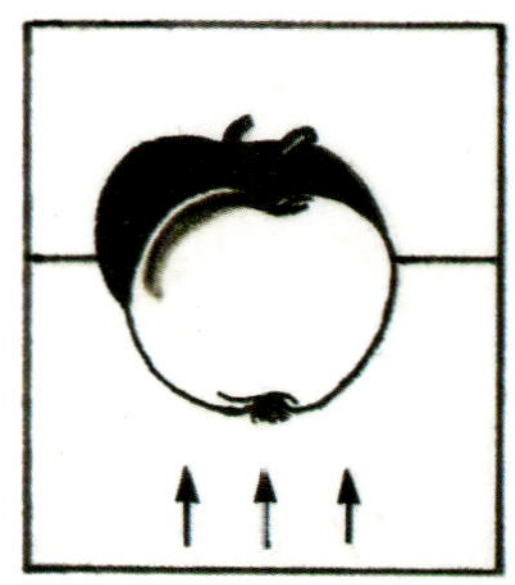

Where is the light coming from?

LIGHT AND SHADE

Some very powerful imagery can be created with the clever use of light and shadow — and the quality of light and shade is one of the major characteristics that separate one group of painters from another. Australian landscape paintings, for instance, are distinguished from European landscapes by the brilliant clear light. European painters are more familiar with overcast skies. Painters of the 16th and 17th centuries were used to interiors lit with the warm, yellowish glow of candlelight and you can see this quite clearly in their paintings.

Just as light can have different qualities, so can shadow — from solid, velvety black, to the palest smokey grey. The Impressionists showed us that shade is the opposite colour to the colour of light — yellow sunlight casts a purple shadow.

Shadows give substance to form, and the positions of the shadows indicate the whereabouts of the sources of light.

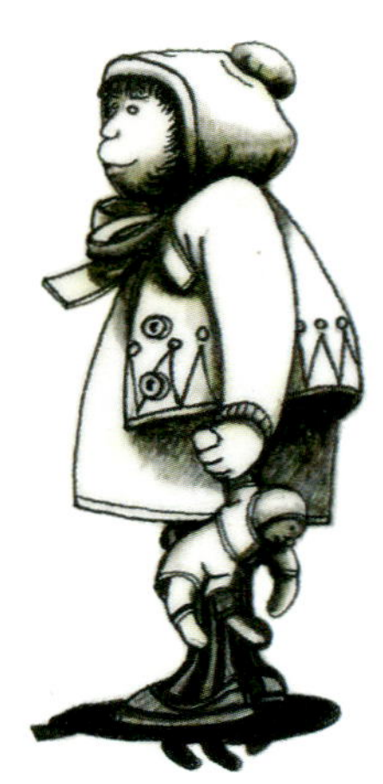

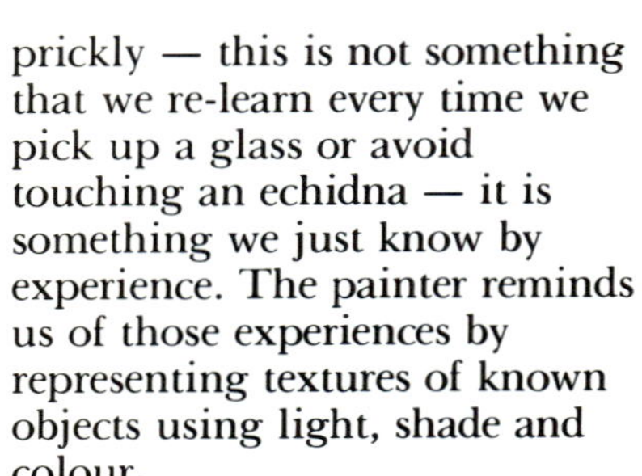

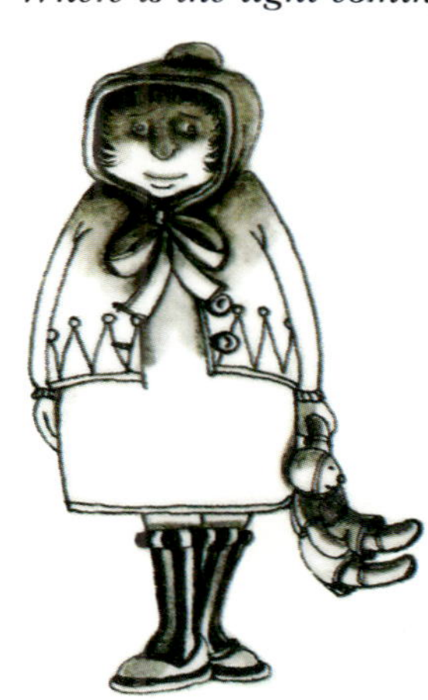

TEXTURE

How does the artist convey the feel of something?

Simulated texture

Firstly, the artist relies on people's memories. Everyone knows, for instance, that glass is smooth and that echidnas are prickly — this is not something that we re-learn every time we pick up a glass or avoid touching an echidna — it is something we just know by experience. The painter reminds us of those experiences by representing textures of known objects using light, shade and colour.

Actual texture

Secondly, the artist can build in a texture to the painting with swirls of lumpy, thick paint or with additions of glue and sand, so that if you were to reach out and touch the painting, it would have a very distinctive 'feel'.

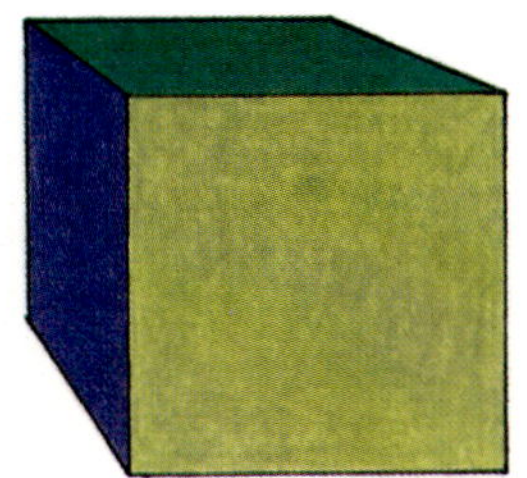

COLOUR

When you think of blue what colour do you see in your mind? A thin watery blue, the brilliant blue of a sapphire or the soft blue-black of the night sky? There are so many different variations of every hue, and they all create a different impression.

Colours interact with each other, and the effects of this interaction depend on the sizes of the areas of the colour, as well as the relationship of one colour to another.

How are colours related?
All colours are made up from three primary colours, red, yellow and blue. An infinite range of colours or of 'hues' can be made by mixing any two primaries in varying proportions (except browns, which are a mixture of all three). Add to this shadings of black or grey or tints of white and you have an infinite variety of 'tone'.

The relationship of colours to one another is best demonstrated by this colour wheel. 'Harmonious' colours are colours based on hues that are neighbours on the colour wheel and tend towards subtle, restful effects, while 'complementary' colours (colours from the opposite sides of the wheel) have a dynamic, disturbing effect.

All painters have their own preferred colour selection, as individual as their handwriting.

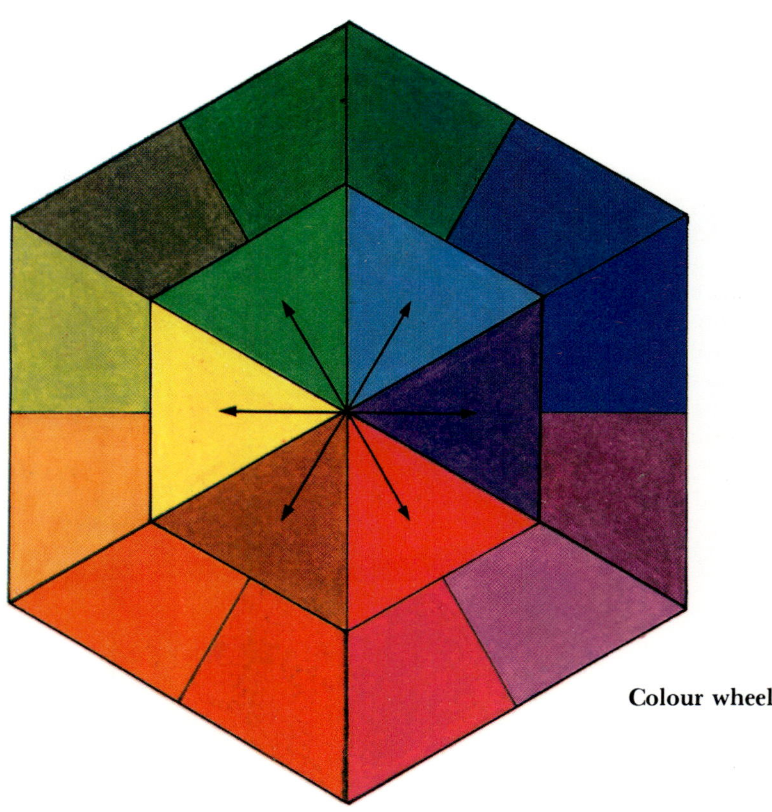

Colour wheel

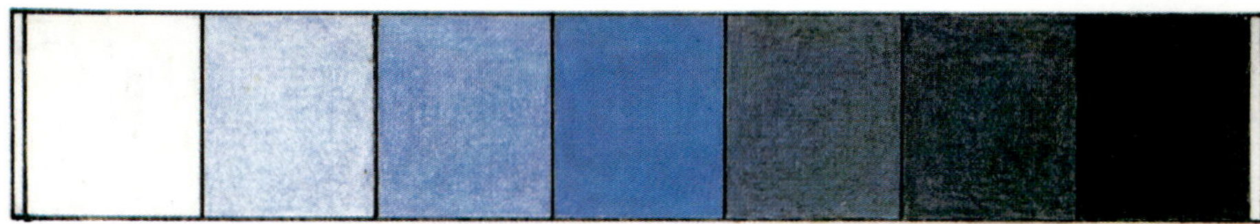

Different tones of one blue

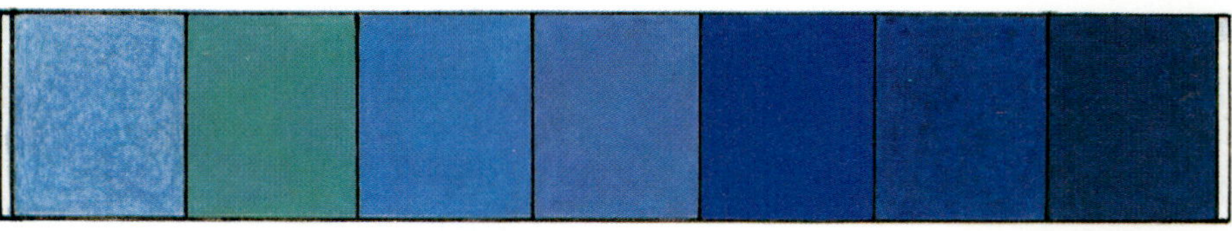

Different hues of blue

COMPOSITION

One of the artist's main tasks is to arrange all the elements in the picture in a way that best conveys his or her intention. The artist may want a balanced picture with the main subject, placed to capture attention, right in the middle. On the other hand, a picture may convey its message better if the main focus of attention is off to one side.

There is a lot to consider when planning a picture — not only the colours, sizes and shapes but also the spaces in between.

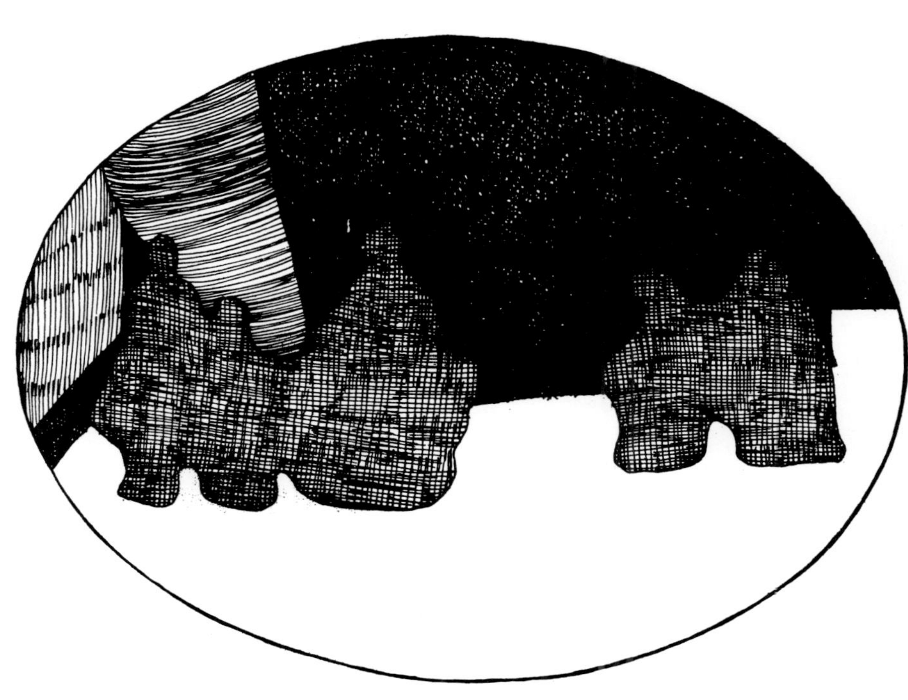

This is a diagram showing the composition of one of the paintings in the first part of this book. Can you guess which painting it is? Take some tracing paper and block out the composition of some of the other paintings.

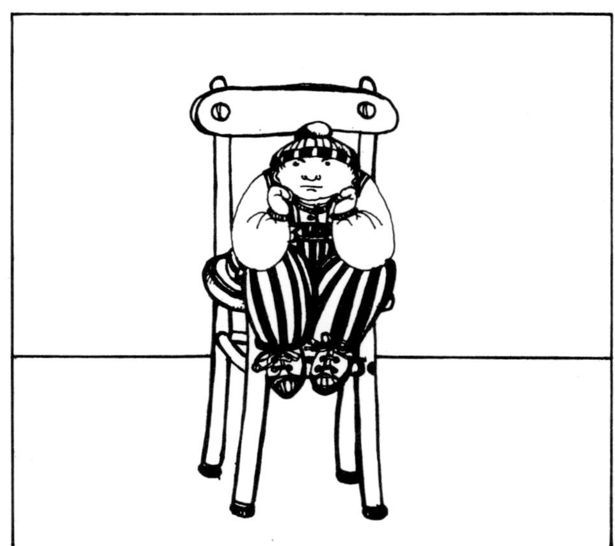

Here's an example of a balanced composition. The subject is right in the middle. Not much is going on — it's a bit boring really.

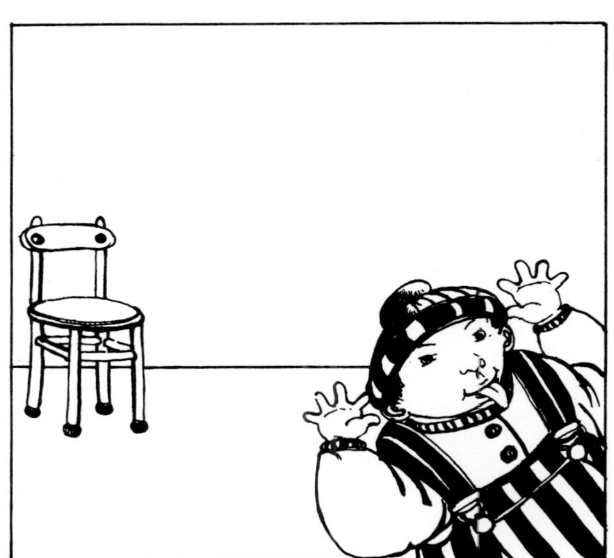

This drawing is still of a little boy and a chair, but in this one the focus of attention is off to one side. Maybe the artist feels that this is the best way to show us the cheeky character of the little boy.

IDEAS

Painting a picture is not about faithfully representing the original. You might as well take a photograph if that's all you want.
A painting or drawing is a personal vision, and every artist sees things in a different way.

Take for instance a simple subject — The Cat. One artist may see a tiger stalking through the undergrowth: menacing, teeth bared, eyes glaring. Another may see a pampered domestic pet. Another may be more interested in the cat's markings, and get carried away with patterns and shapes. Yet another may see the cat as a cartoon character, taking on human characteristics.

They are all, in their very different, individual ways, telling you what they see when they think of cats.

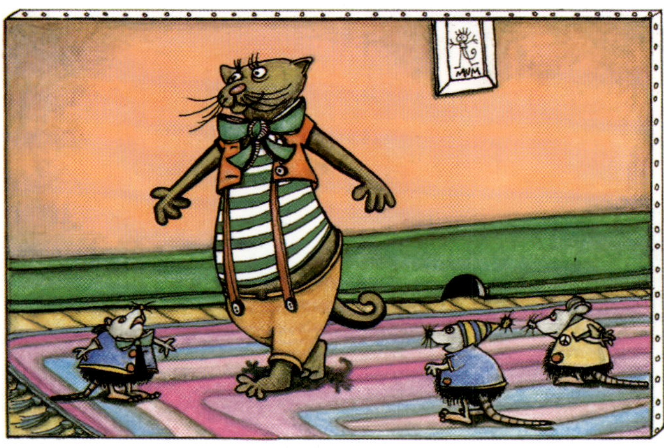

The Cat *by A. Painter*

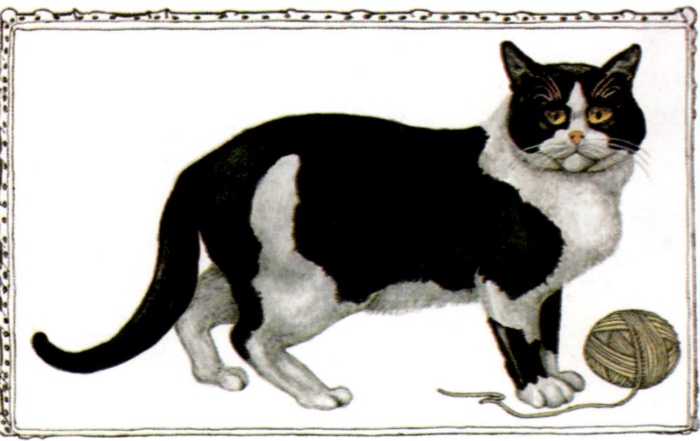

The Cat *by B. Painter*

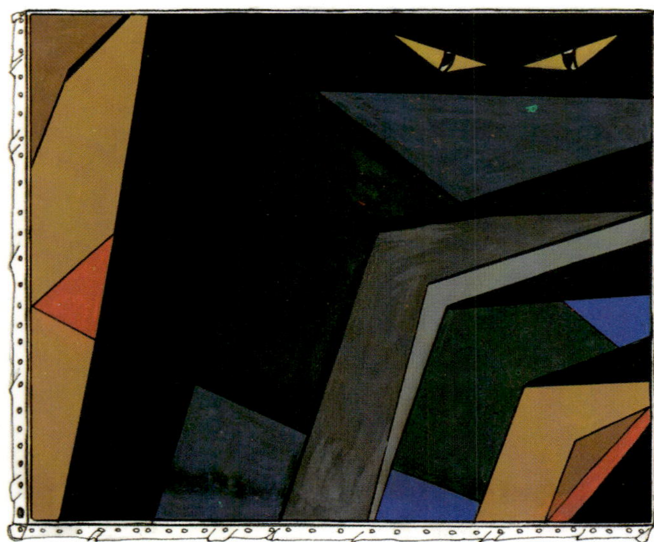

The Cat *by C. Painter*

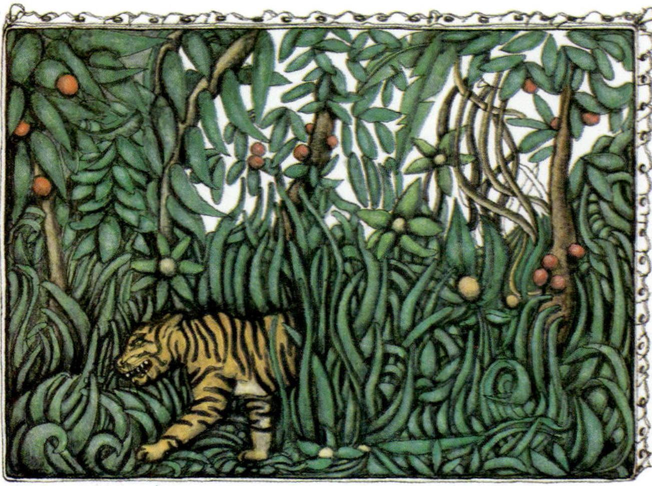

The Cat *by D. Painter.*

THE MATERIALS OF ART

Every kind of paint, pencil and painting surface has its own possibilities and its own limits, and artists will choose materials that are best suited to the image they have in mind.

PAINTING

Basically, all paints are made of 'pigment' or powdered colour mixed with something that will bind the powder and make it stick to the painting surface. Pigments are either made chemically or (less often, these days) from naturally-coloured substances such as earth, minerals and plants. It is the stuff that binds the powdered pigment together that determines the paint's characteristics.

The most common types of paint are:

Oil-paint This is the most versatile and subtle of all. It dries slowly so it can be used to blend layers of tone and colour and it can be built up with glazes of thin colour to give a translucent sheen. Most pigments used in oil paints are not transparent and they do not change colour as they dry. Oil paint can be applied in thick layers to create interesting textures. This technique is called 'Impasto'.

Tempera The word tempera originally applied to all paints that had been 'tempered', or mixed with something to make the pigment stick. Nowadays we use the term tempera to describe pigment mixed with the yolk of an egg and thinned with water. Tempera is very fast-drying, and gives a precise, clear line and a rather flat effect. But it is a difficult medium to work with and not well-suited to subjects that demand feelings of depth or shadow.

Watercolours are made from very finely-ground pigment that has been bound with a sticky resin called gum arabic and then thinned with water. Watercolour applied to white paper is simple to use and can produce a wonderful translucent effect because the light reflects back from the paper through the colour.

Gouache is also made from pigment bound with gum arabic and thinned with water, but the mix is different. The paint is thicker and not transparent. Gouache, sometimes called poster paint, is easy to use and quick-drying. It is commonly used on flat, rigid surfaces, as it is very inflexible and would crack and flake off a bendy surface like canvas.

Acrylic These paints are really refinements of industrial paints, and are made from pigment bound with a man-made resin. They are easy to handle, can be thinned with water and applied to almost any surface by almost any method, from a spray gun to a shovel. Acrylic paint is the only really new paint to have been invented in the past 500 years or so. The results look very similar to oil paint, but acrylic paint dries much faster.

DRAWING

Ink Principally used for line work, ink is a major factor in oriental art. Artists use either Indian ink or Sepia. Indian ink is black. It is made from wood or vegetable soot mixed with animal glue and diluted with water — the less water, the blacker the ink. Sepia, which is extracted from cuttlefish, is a lovely shade of brown.

Pastel chalks are made of pure pigment mixed to a paste with a little resin and then dried. The colours are wonderfully intense but pastel is very crumbly to work with.

Charcoal or charred wood was the first drawing implement known to artists. It gives a range of different effects from thin, sharp lines to smokey smudges, but it is very difficult to keep a charcoal drawing clean and free from unintentional smudges.

Pencil Lead pencils are made from powdered graphite, which comes in varying degrees of softness decribed as Hard (H) or Black (B) — so a **4H** pencil gives an extremely fine, thin line, while a **4B** is soft and smudgy.

Crayons are made from pigment mixed with wax and bound with gum. They are extremely easy to use but rather limited in the range of effects as you can always see the strokes of the crayon.

THE SURFACE

Canvas is a woven linen material which, when stretched on to a wooden frame and sealed or primed with an undercoat of special white paint makes an excellent surface for oil paints, acrylics and tempera. The soft, woven surface makes it ideal for building up all sorts of textures.

Paper Paper can be made out of many different things. In Asia they make thin white paper (often called rice paper) from vegetable pulp and leaves, while the Ancient Egyptians used the broad papyrus reeds of the river Nile to write on. Today most paper is made from wood pulp which has been treated with acid to help break it down, and then rolled out flat. But art paper is usually made from pulped and rolled linen rags. It can withstand constant wetting, making it suitable for watercolours. To prevent the paper from crinkling, it is either 'stretched' or pasted onto thin card.

Board A lot of early paintings were done on wooden boards made into panels. The flat, smooth surface had to be primed or sealed before use.

Today, board usually means either canvas board (canvas pasted onto cardboard) or art board which is a kind of cardboard with a specially-treated surface.

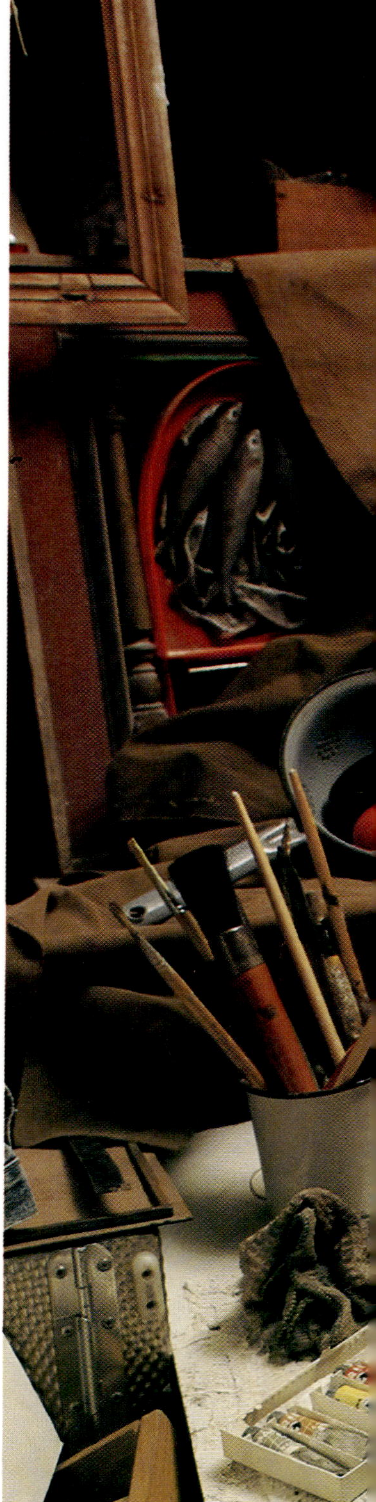

The studio of photographer and artist Lewis Morley.

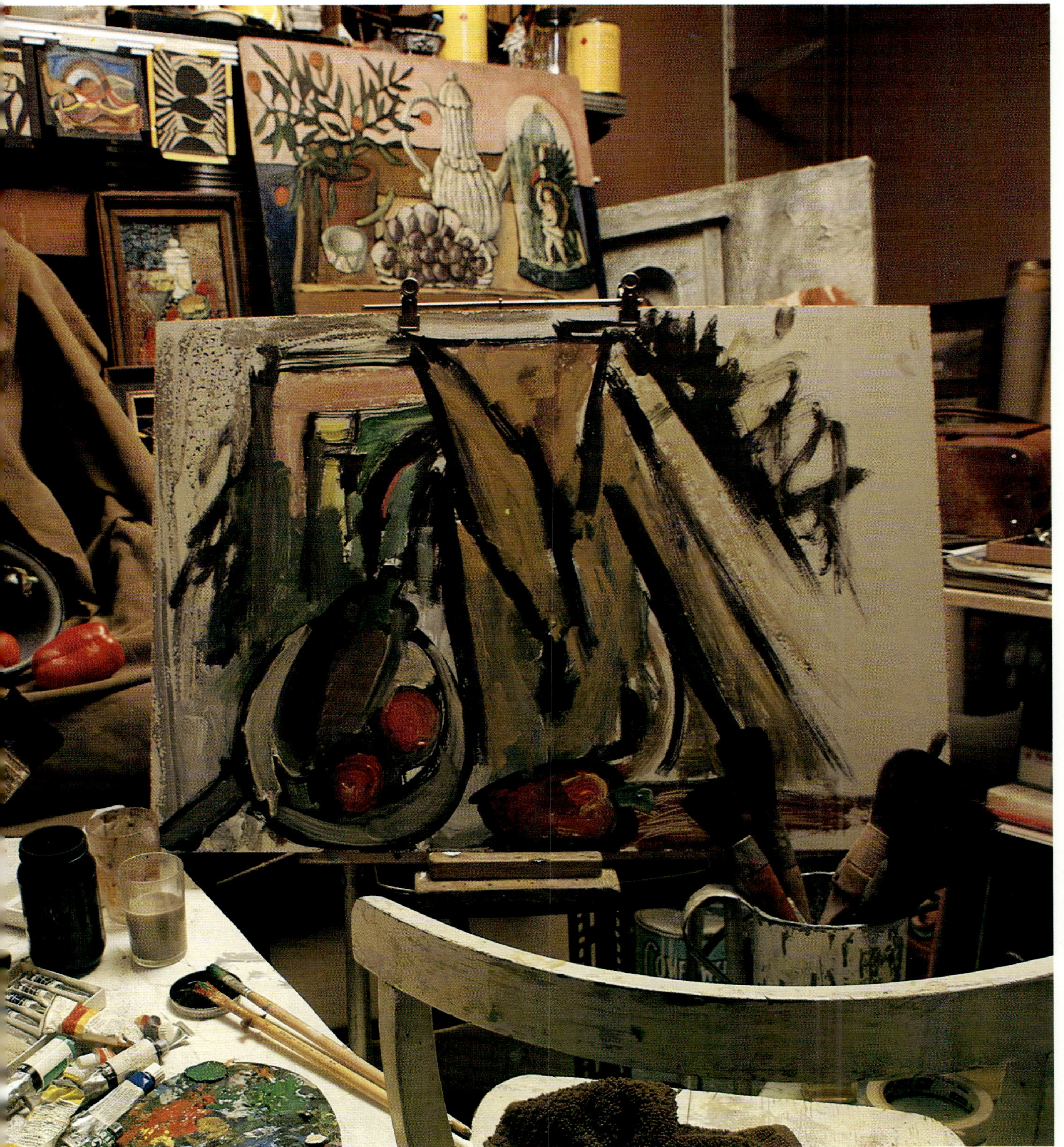

PRINT MAKING

Today, limited edition prints are regarded as works of art in their own right — not just copies of originals. Many artists work with print because it gives certain effects that cannot be achieved by other means.

There are three basic types of print:

1 Relief

Wood cuts and lino cuts are the most common examples of relief printing, in which the areas not to be printed are cut away.

A wood block — *an example of relief printing*

2 Engraving

This method is the reverse of relief printing. The lines that are to be inked are cut away, and the special press used for this process forces the paper into the grooves to pick up the ink.

3 Surface printing

A typical surface printing method is lithography, in which the design is drawn directly on to a stone or a metal plate with an oily paint or greasy pencil. After this has been done, water is put on the surface.

As oil and water don't mix, the design remains dry and the blank parts of the plate get wet. An oil-based ink is then rolled on to the plate which sticks only to the greasy drawing (the dry bits). Coloured lithographs are made up of several separate plates — one for each colour.

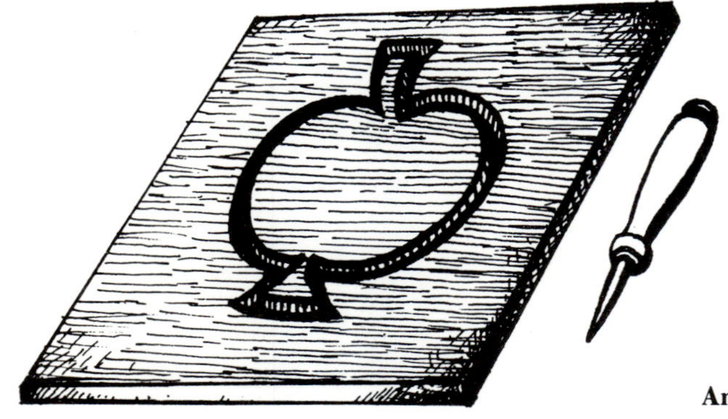

An engraved metal plate

A three-colour lithograph

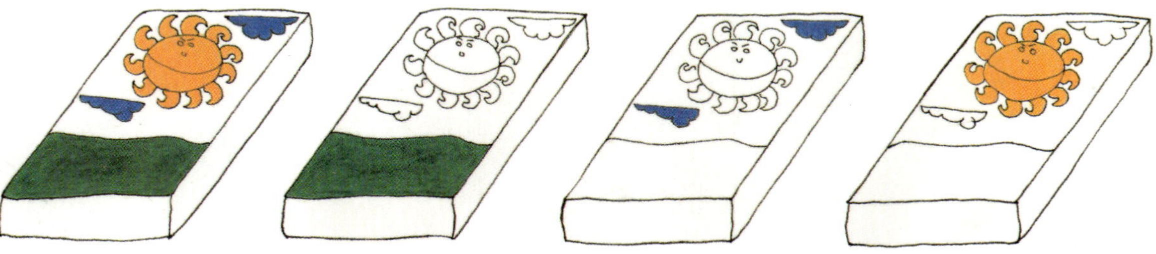

MULTIMEDIA

Today's artists, freed from the old traditions, can express their ideas using not just a painting surface, a brush and a box of paints, but any ingredients that come to hand, such as glue and nails, coloured fabric and old bicycle wheels. They also cross the barriers into other art forms such as photography, poetry or film so that art really does reflect our everyday experiences.

An assemblage by Lewis Morley.

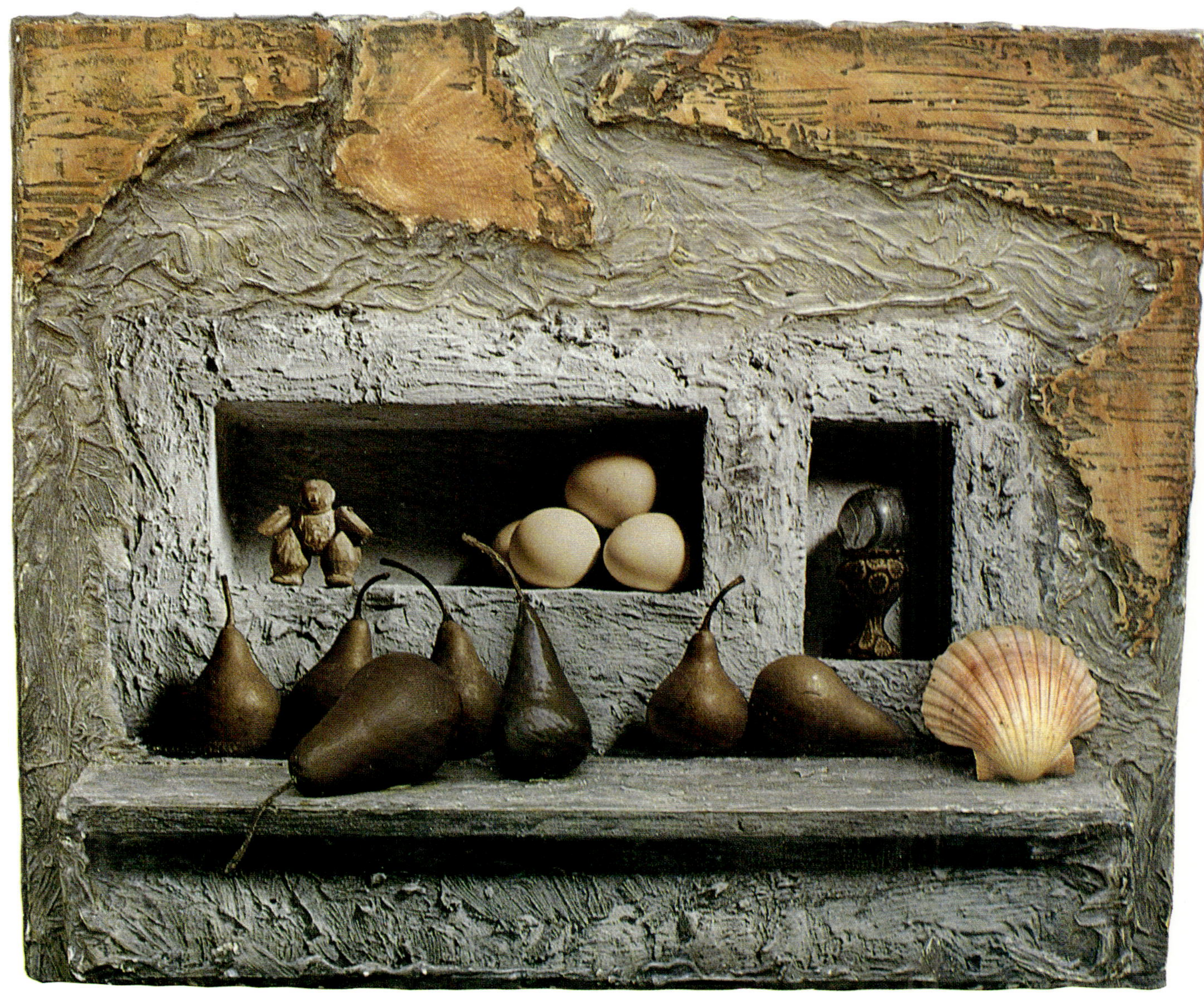

VICTORIA

National Gallery of Victoria
180 St Kilda Road
Melbourne 3000
Contact: Education Officer
Tel: (03) 618 0222

RMIT Faculty Gallery
Building 2
342-348 Swanston Street
Melbourne 3000
Tel: (03) 662 0611

Print Council of Australia
105 Collins Street
Melbourne 3000
Tel: (03) 654 2460

Victorian College of the Arts
Exhibitions Gallery
234 St Kilda Road
Melbourne 3004
Tel: (03) 616 9300

Performing Arts Museum
Victoria Arts Centre
100 St Kilda Road
Melbourne 3004
Tel: (03) 617 8211

Melbourne University Gallery
Parkville 3052
Tel: (03) 344 6961

Grainger Museum
University of Melbourne
Parkville 3052
Tel: (03) 344 5270

Gertrude Street Artist Spaces Inc.
188 Gertrude Street
Fitzroy 3065
Tel: (03) 419 3406

Banyule Gallery
60 Buckingham Drive
Heidelberg 3084
Tel: (03) 459 7899

Heide Park & Art Gallery
7 Templestowe Road
Bulleen 3105
Tel: (03) 850 1849

Hawthorn City Art Gallery
584 Glenferrie Road
Hawthorn 3122
Tel: (03) 819 2444

Waverley City Gallery
14 The Highway
Mt Waverley 3149
Tel: (03) 277 7261

Caulfield Art Centre
441 Inkerman Road
Caulfield 3162
Tel: (03) 524 3277

Exhibition Gallery
Monash University
Wellington Road
Clayton 3168
Tel: (03) 669 8666

Geelong Art Gallery
Little Malop Street
Geelong 3220
Tel: (052) 21 7877

Warrnambool Art Gallery
214 Timor Street
Warrnambool 3280
Tel: (055) 62 9920

City of Hamilton Art Gallery
Brown Street
Hamilton 3300
Tel: (055) 73 0460

Ballarat Fine Art Gallery
40 Lydiard Street North
Ballarat 3350
Tel: (053) 31 5622

Ararat Gallery
Town Hall
Vincent Street
Ararat 3377
Tel: (053) 52 2836

Horsham Regional Art Gallery
Town Hall Building
80 Wilson Street
Horsham 3400
Tel: (053) 82 5575

Castlemaine Art Gallery
Lyttleton Street
Castlemaine 3450
Tel: (054) 72 2292

Mildura Arts Centre
199 Cureton Avenue
Mildura 3500
Tel: (050) 23 3733

Bendigo Art Gallery
View Street
Bendigo 3550
Tel: (054) 43 4491

Swan Hill Regional Art Gallery
Pioneer Settlement
Swan Hill 3585
Tel: (050) 32 1403

Shepparton Arts Centre
Civic Centre
Welsford Street
Shepparton 3630
Tel: (058) 21 6352

Benalla Art Gallery
Bridge Street
Benalla 3672
Tel: (057) 62 3833

La Trobe Valley Arts Centre
138 Commercial Road
Morwell 3840
Tel: (051) 34 1364

Sale Region Arts Centre
Macalister Street
Sale 3850
Tel: (051) 44 2829

McClelland Gallery
McClelland Drive
Langwarren 3910
Tel: (03) 789 1671

Mornington Peninsula Arts Centre
4 Vancouver Street
Mornington 3931
Tel: (059) 75 4395

NEW SOUTH WALES

Art Gallery of NSW
Art Gallery Road
The Domain
Sydney 2000
Contact: Education Officer
Tel: (02) 225 1700

Mint & Hyde Park Barracks
Queens Square
Macquarie Street
Sydney 2000
Tel: (02) 217 0111

SH Ervin Museum & Art Gallery
National Trust Centre
Observatory Hill
Sydney 2000
Tel: (02) 27 9222
      (02) 275374

Power Institue of Contemporary Art Gallery
University of Sydney
Sydney 2006
Tel: (02) 692 3170

Ivan Dougherty Gallery
Sydney College of Advanced
Education Cnr Albion Avenue &
Selwyn Street
Paddington 2021
Tel: (02) 339 9555

Manly Art Gallery
West Esplanade Reserve
Manly 2095
Tel: (02) 949 2435

Gosford City Art Collection
49 Mann Street
Gosford 2250
Tel: (043) 24 2811

Lake Macquarie Community Art Centre Gallery
Old Council Chambers
Boolaroo 2284
Tel: (049) 58 0459
      (049) 58 5333

Newcastle Region Art Gallery
Laman Street
Newcastle 2300
Tel: (049) 26 3644

Port Stephens Society of the Arts
Cultural Centre
Shoal Bay Road
Nelson Bay 2315
Tel: (049) 81 3604

Maitland City Art Gallery
Brough House
Church Street
Maitland 2320
Tel: (049) 33 1657

Muswellbrook Regional Art Gallery
Bridge Street
Muswellbrook 2333
Tel: (065) 43 3984

Tamworth City Art Gallery
Marius Street
Tamworth 2340
Tel: (067) 66 2280

New England Regional Art Museum
Kentucky Street
Armidale 2350
Tel: (067) 72 5255

Taree Municipal Council Art Collection
Taree Municipal Council
Pulteney Street
Taree 2430
Tel: (065) 52 1126

Coffs Harbour Shire Council
Cnr Coff & Castle Streets
Coffs Harbour 2450
Tel: (066) 52 2555

Grafton City Council
2 Prince Street
Grafton 2460
Tel: (066) 42 2266

Albury Regional Art Centre
Dean Street
Albury 2640
Tel: (060) 21 6384

Wagga Wagga City Art Gallery
Gurwood Street
Wagga Wagga 2650
Tel: (069) 21 3621

Lismore Regional Art Gallery
Molesworth Street
Lismore 2480
Tel: (066) 21 1536

Wollongong City Art Gallery
Cnr Keira & Burrelli Streets
Wollongong East 2500
Tel: (042) 28 7802

Shoalhaven City Council
Bridge Road
Nowra 2540
Tel: (044) 21 6011

Bega Valley Shire Council
Zingel Place
Bega 2550
Tel: (0649) 2 1088

Goulburn Regional Art Gallery
Sloane Street
Goulburn 2580
Tel: (048) 21 1444

ACT

Australian National Gallery
Parkes Place
Canberra Parkes 2601
Contact: Education Officer
Tel: (062) 71 2411

Australian War Memorial
Canberra 2600
Tel: (062) 43 4211

Arts Council of Australia Gallery
Gorman House
Ainslie Avenue
Braddon 2601

Tel: (062) 48 9813

Canberra School of Art Gallery
Baldessin Crescent
Canberra 2601
Tel: (062) 46 7946

Nolan Gallery
Lanyon Homestead
Tharwa
Canberra 2601
Tel: (062) 37 5192

Bitumen River Gallery
Cnr Furneaux
& Bougainville Streets
Manuka
Canberra 2603
Tel: (062) 95 7319

Griffith Regional Art Gallery
167 Banna Avenue
Griffith 2680
Tel: (069) 62 5991

**Lewers Penrith Regional
Art Gallery**
87 River Road
Emu Plains 2750
Tel: (047) 35 1448

Bathurst Regional Art Gallery
Civic Centre
Bathurst 2795
Tel: (063) 33 6283

Orange Civic Centre Gallery
Byng Street
Orange 2800
Tel: (063) 62 1755

Dubbo City Council
Church Street
Dubbo 2830
Tel: (068) 82 2211

Broken Hill City Art Gallery
Chloride Street
Broken Hill 2880
Tel: (080) 6602

QUEENSLAND

Queensland Art Gallery
Cnr Melbourne & Grey Streets
South Brisbane 4101
Contact: Education Officer
Tel: (07) 240 7333

Institute of Modern Art
106 Edward Street
Brisbane 4000
Tel: (07) 229 5985

**Brisbane City Civic Art Gallery &
Museum**
City Hall
Brisbane 4000
Tel: (07) 221 1507

University Art Museum
University of Queensland
St Lucia 4067
Tel: (07) 377 3048

Queensland College of Art Gallery
Foxton Street
Morningside 4170
Tel: (07) 395 9100

Toowoomba City Art Gallery
Ruthven Street
Toowoomba 4350
Tel: (076) 379 5500

Bundaberg Art Collection
Bourbong Street
Bundaberg 4670
Tel: (071) 72 3700

Rockhampton Art Gallery
City Hall
Rockhampton 4700
Tel: (079) 27 7129

SOUTH AUSTRALIA

Art Gallery of South Australia
North Terrace
Adelaide 5000
Contact: Education Officer
Tel: (08) 223 7200

Flinders University Art Gallery
Sturt Road
Bedford Park 5042
Tel: (08) 275 3911

**Contemporary Art Society
of Australia**
14 Porter Street
Parkside 5063
Tel: (08) 272 2682

Naracoorte Art Gallery
128 Smith Street
Naracoorte 5271
Tel: (087) 62 1636

Riddoch Art Gallery
Civic Centre
Watson Terrace
Mt Gambier 5290
Tel: (087) 24 1572

NORTHERN TERRITORY

**Museums & Art Galleries
of Northern Territory**
Star Village
Smith Street Mall
Darwin 5794
Tel: (089) 81 6488

Araleun Arts & Cultural Trust
Larapinta Drive
Alice Springs 5750
Tel: (089) 52 5022

WESTERN AUSTRALIA

Art Gallery of Western Australia
47 James Street
Perth 6000
Contact: Education Officer
Tel: (09) 328 7233

Undercroft Gallery
University of Western Australia
Nedlands 6009
Tel: (09) 380 2006

**Western Australia Insitute
of Technology**
Heyman Street
South Bentley 6102
Tel: (09) 350 7700

Fremantle Arts Centre
1 Finnerty Street
Fremantle 6160
Tel: (09) 335 8244

Bunbury Art Gallery
Princep Street
Bunbury 6230
Tel: (097) 21 6173

Albany Art Gallery
Town Council
Albany 6330
Tel: (098) 41 5824

Derby Art Gallery
Derby Cultural Centre
Derby 6728
Tel: (091) 91 1443

TASMANIA

Tasmanian Museum & Art Gallery
5 Argyle Street
Hobart 7001
Contact: Education Officer
Tel: (002) 23 1422

Tasmanian School of Art Gallery
Olinda Street
Mount Nelson 7007
Tel: (002) 20 3133

Burnie Art Gallery
Wilmot Street
Burnie 7230
Tel: (004) 31 5918

**Queen Victoria Museum
& Art Gallery**
Wellington Street
Launceston 7250
Tel: (003) 31 6777

Devonport Gallery
Steel Street
Devonport 7310
Tel: (004) 24 0561

INDEX/ACKNOWLEDGEMENTS

ACKNOWLEDGEMENTS
The publishers would like to thank the following for their invaluable help:
Phillip Jago *National Gallery of Victoria,*
Lance Cosgrove *Tasmanian Museum & Art Gallery,*
Pamela Laycock *New England Regional Art Museum,*
Terence Measham, Elizabeth Bilney and Jane Hayden *Australian National Gallery,*
Anna Waldmann *Art Gallery of New South Wales,*
Geoff Easton *The Art Gallery of Western Australia,*
Caroline Launitz-Schurer and Janet Hogan *Queensland Art Gallery,*
Helen Tyzack *Newcastle Region Art Gallery,*
Catherine Roberts *Art Gallery of South Australia,*
With extra special thanks to Elwyn Lynn, Claude Parsons and James Somerled